T0114131

Cambridge Elements ≡

Elements in Publishing and Book Culture
edited by
Samantha Rayner
University College London
Leah Tether
University of Bristol

UNDERDEVELOPMENT AND AFRICAN LITERATURE

Emerging Forms of Reading

Sarah Brouillette

Carleton University

CAMBRIDGE
UNIVERSITY PRESS

CAMBRIDGE
UNIVERSITY PRESS

University Printing House, Cambridge CB2 8BS, United Kingdom

One Liberty Plaza, 20th Floor, New York, NY 10006, USA

477 Williamstown Road, Port Melbourne, VIC 3207, Australia

314–321, 3rd Floor, Plot 3, Splendor Forum, Jasola District Centre,
New Delhi – 110025, India

79 Anson Road, #06–04/06, Singapore 079906

Cambridge University Press is part of the University of Cambridge.

It furthers the University's mission by disseminating knowledge in the pursuit of
education, learning, and research at the highest international levels of excellence.

www.cambridge.org
Information on this title: www.cambridge.org/9781108713788
DOI: 10.1017/9781108624947

First published 2020

A catalogue record for this publication is available from the British Library.

ISBN 978-1-108-71378-8 Paperback
ISSN 2514-8524 (online)
ISSN 2514-8516 (print)

Underdevelopment and African Literature

Emerging Forms of Reading

Elements in Publishing and Book Culture

DOI: 10.1017/9781108624947
First published online: December 2020

Sarah Brouillette

Carleton University

Author for correspondence: Sarah Brouillette, sarah_brouillette@carleton.ca

ABSTRACT: People looking for work in cities are immersed in English as the lingua franca of the mobile phone and the urban hustle – more effective instigations to reading than decades of work by traditional publishers and development agencies. The legal publishing industry campaigns to convince people to scorn pirates and plagiarists as a criminal underclass, and to instead purchase copyrighted, barcoded works that have the look of legitimacy about them. They work with development industry officials to "foster literacy" – meaning to grow the legal book trade as a contributor to national economic health, and police what and how the newly literate read. But harried cash-strapped audiences will read what and how they can, often outside of formal economies, and are increasingly turning to mobile phone platforms that sell texts at a fraction of the price of legally printed books.

KEYWORDS: African literatures, publishing studies, cultural sociology, cultural studies, literary studies

ISBNs: 9781108713788 (PB), 9781108624947 (OC)
ISSNs: 2514-8524 (online), 2514-8516 (print)

Contents

1 Introduction

This study offers an approach to contemporary English-language African reading culture, surveying and synthesizing the substantial body of fascinating research that exists on the topic. I provide an overview of the history of underdevelopment of postcolonial publishing, with a focus on the period of economic turbulence and immiseration since the 1970s, before then moving to the contemporary situation, from about the turn of the twenty-first century to the present. Homing in on Nigeria and Kenya, with some comments extending to Zimbabwe, Uganda, and South Africa as relevant comparisons, I discuss both the elite literary sphere and more demotic popular forms of reading activity, and consider the relationships between these fields: between, that is, an established coterie of African writers that finds a sizable readership abroad, and a less literary local reading culture whose materials are ephemeral and habits hard to trace, and whose fate is tied – in ways I attempt to understand – to urbanization and to the realities of underemployment and labor informality.

I argue here that it is useful to think somewhat schematically, much as Pierre Bourdieu once did when thinking about the literary field in France, which he separated into two "fields," one restricted and autonomous, with players possessing high prestige, and the other large-scale and heteronomous, where players are more interested in wealth and capitalization of increasing production. I suggest that these terms are not quite sufficient now, however – not just for the study of English-language publishing in Africa, but for the study of contemporary literary culture in general. We should highlight a different split instead, between a vibrant, dynamic, entrepreneurial culture of reading that has arisen as an offshoot of practical, material pressure to learn English, and a more established literary culture that imagines itself as activism and uplift. An African literary milieu would like to cultivate a local readership, but it also has access to foreign markets and private donors in order to facilitate its ongoing stability. I argue that the more dynamic popular culture is usefully thought of as picaresque, lacking a sustained engagement in aspirational culture or the goal of expansion of legal trades; the more high-literary elite culture is, on the other hand, still very much invested in the bildung of improvement and expansion. Like

Bourdieu again, the point is not to suggest that these spheres exist in isolation from one another, but rather precisely to consider how they are inseparable, gaining meaning only in that relation. Bourdieu emphasized that accruing cultural capital often meant disavowing the actual making of money, and that those with existing wealth were more readily able to position themselves as autonomous cultural producers. Here, differently, I stress that the funded high-literary sphere exists in part to discipline and manage more popular forms of reading in English, especially those forms that do little to expand legal publishing infrastructure.

Following this brief introduction, Section 2 contains an overview and explanation of my basic premises. I provide cautions about the value attached to literacy in English, arguing that it might reflect immiseration rather than "development" as generally defined by the agencies that monitor literacy statistics. I suggest English literacy be considered a tool taken on out of material necessity, which is expanding not alongside prospects for human development but rather in lockstep with urbanization and immiseration. Section 3 surveys the study of English-language publishing in the former colonies, and is focused on the relationship between learning English and social mobility and the oft-lamented fact of the relatively small leisure-reading audience, with people tending to stop reading much at all after formal schooling. I highlight some of the more significant schemes that Western firms developed to exploit markets for school textbooks within Africa – namely the Heinemann African Writers Series and Oxford University Press's Three Crowns Series. I also suggest how study of African literature has dealt with ongoing relations of neocolonial dependence within the industry, in which many aspiring literary writers perceive a need to write in English, to have contracts with foreign firms, or to write with foreign audiences in mind, if they want to achieve success.

My fourth section then moves the discussion closer to the present, connecting contemporary conditions to the history of underdevelopment of the publishing industries in Africa. I discuss some of the ways in which African writers have bypassed the absent local reader, and emphasize the crucial role played by US-private foundation funding in the ongoing viability of the African literary scene. Section 5 considers a short story, "Jumping Money Hill" by Chimamanda Adichie. I read this story, which is a fascinating skewering of a writing workshop, in relation to the power of foundation-funded literary writing workshops within the African literary milieu. I argue that the story is an effort to ground Adichie's own authority within that scene, and I offer my reading of it as an example of the way that understanding institutional conditions can help illuminate literature's meanings.

Section 6 then turns to what I describe as more demotic picaresque forms, or those entrepreneurial sites of reading production that are more motivated by immediate necessity and less intent on expansion of legal production of reading materials, especially high literary ones. I trace a number of these forms, including texts for smartphones and pirated books. Section 7 then highlights some relationships between the high-literary sphere and the demotic sphere, via another kind of close reading, this time of volunteer reports by people involved with the Canadian Organization for Development through Education (CODE) Burt Literary Awards, which aim at expanding young adult readership. I look at the developmentalist mindset within these reports, as they search submitted manuscripts for particular literary values, such as completeness, cohesion, and evidence of substantive editing. I consider the qualities of one recent winning title, *Finding Colombia* (2018), whose protagonist is entrapped by the police into catching a notorious drug lord, and I look then at the efforts of his publisher, Oxford University Press East Africa, to clamp down on book piracy by hailing readers as people similarly eager to stop criminals. Drawing on the work of Esther de Bruijn, I then compare *Finding Colombia* to a book she has studied wonderfully, called *The Wicked Mother* – a more ephemeral piece of informal market literature that does not meet the standards of the legal book trade, but that no doubt offered its readers some important skills and pleasures. In the final section I conclude by expanding on this comparison, suggesting that the legal developmentalist trade is motivated to try to capture and in fact discipline some of the dynamism and vibrancy of the more street-level picaresque reading culture that is, for understandable reasons, less respectful of private property rights.

This is a brief Element; my treatment is synthetic and suggestive rather than comprehensive and complete. I hope nevertheless that it might encourage some interesting new ways to think about literary culture in English as it is emerging today.

2 English as Immiseration

It is impossible to estimate with much accuracy how many people are literate in English in Africa; and it is important to challenge the idea that only one form of activity counts as literacy, or that only something like "full" literacy should stand as an official measure. Official literacy statistics measure ability both to read and to write a simple sentence. Yet often people who are semiliterate can read but not write, and those whose abilities are unknown, because they have not been surveyed, are not counted in the statistics. We could surmise then that one recent English Proficiency Index estimate that the rate for Africa as a whole is approximately 50.28 percent is probably low (EF 2020a). It is likely that more people can read in English than can write in it, and there are more people now learning to read in English outside of formal schools, and therefore outside of the catchment group for any proficiency surveying, as they seek informal work in cities.

Nor should we accept, of course, the notion that literate culture is measurably distinct from and superior to oral culture. On the contrary, as many writers have argued, there is little reason to try to separate categorically orality from literacy – efforts to do so have usually been hugely ideologically suspect – while clearly the activity of writing things down is only one mode of creative expression among many, with its own affordances and limitations. In Stephanie Newell's words, "presence of one or two book-reading individuals in a small community is sufficient for textual interpretations and printed opinions to circulate widely among non-literate people"; and oral performers often know and play with established literary genres and tropes (2006, 71). The fetish for literacy and for printed objects is itself a symptom of a developmentalist ethos that promotes nation building, economic development, and integration into productive employment. This ethos infects much of the research on reading in English in Africa, and it is one that we need to treat critically if we want to see the situation clearly.

For while literacy is, as part of this ethos, included in all the official measures of a nation's development, there are several respects in which this is deceiving. In the African locations I focus on here, which are for the most part sub-Saharan urban enclaves where people read texts in English, there is under- and overdevelopment, poverty and wealth, slums and wealthy gated communities side by side. To quote a recent piece by economic historian Aaron Benanav: "Our present reality is better described by near-future science-fiction dystopias than by standard economic analysis; ours is a hot planet, with micro-drones flying over the heads of the street hawkers and rickshaw pullers, where the rich live in guarded, climate-controlled communities while the rest of us wile away our time in dead-end jobs, playing video games on smartphones" (2019, 15).

Although there are agents of development still very much trying to usher in social progress linked to endless economic growth, and they make their appearances below, their conventional terminology is something to be studied rather than used without question. Because the truth is not a matter of an intractable syndrome of underdevelopment that helpful development industry experts are trying to ease. Instead the syndrome is the unfolding capitalist present itself, in which that selfsame lionized process, development, in fact ends up serving the real material interests of very few people, while producing and feeding off growing disparities between those possessing relative power and wealth and those who are – in increasing numbers – living in cities and trying to find some sort of fitful employment. These are, moreover, disparities evident not just in Africa but in the places with the economies that we are supposed to think of as "advanced" or "developed" too – places where we also find substantial pockets of underdevelopment and de-development of anything like sufficient supports for human flourishing.

In this light, English literacy may be as much a measure of immiseration as it is a sign of anything like development toward better conditions of life. How does our perspective change if we consider English literacy a kind of tragic consequence of massive social upheaval? A tool taken on through what Pádraig Carmody has suggested we call, in regard to mobile phones, "negative adoption" (2012, 6) – that is, as a result of the sheer force of material necessity? Consider that, even if the literacy percentages remain relatively low compared to other places, the numbers of people are relatively high: the population of Lagos has been estimated at 21 million, up from 1.4 million as recently as 1970. There is in Lagos, as elsewhere in Africa, a so-called youth bulge – an estimated half to two-thirds of the population are under forty years of age, putting pressure on already cash-strapped education systems and inadequate labor markets now and into the future. Statistics from UNESCO for 2018 suggest that 62 percent of Nigerian adults are literate, but 75 percent of young people; one measure of proficiency in English in particular puts the rate for Nigeria at 58.36 (EF 2020b). It is interesting to think then that in Lagos alone there could be more than 10 million present or near future readers, many of them quite young, and this is probably a conservative estimate. Meanwhile rates of use of smartphones, mobile subscriptions, internet access, and social media network use are all on the rise, urged along by the increasing market penetration of cheap Asian phones specifically targeting consumers in Africa. For many young people, the easing of access to phone and mobile networks is reason enough to acquire basic literacy; these technologies are all but essential for survival in precarious conditions, as they connect people to job opportunities and to sometimes life-saving supports offered by family and friends (Dyer-Witheford 2015, 102–123). These technologies also, for book producers, ease some of the burdens associated with establishing a traditional print publishing concern.

Wendy Griswold's pioneering work on reading in Nigeria helpfully drew attention to the very basic conditions that need to be in place for people to develop a serious "reading habit" involving long and relatively difficult books. Habitual readers usually need to find themselves in places where there is "social support for reading, in the form of active encouragement of reading as a highly esteemed activity . . . or at least tolerance of the temporary social withdrawal that reading entails," and "there must be the physical conditions – sufficient light, relative quiet, and some degree of comfortable, personal space – to make sustained reading possible" (2000, 101). Writing in 2000, she wagers that in the absence of these conditions, it is unlikely that regular leisure reading will become much of a pastime for Nigerians, while of course without a substantial readership to sell to there is little incentive for people to try to develop businesses in the book sector. This all makes sense as analysis of the relatively elite reading sector.

We can counter this, however, with a slightly different sociological purview. S. I. A. Kotei's UNESCO-based survey of the state of the book in Africa claims that traditional African social organization is simply against the activity of reading privately. Referring to a "communal syndrome," he laments that only "some people are able to escape the clamour of communality in order to read" (1981, 148). Writing in 1981, he notes that over 70 percent of the African population lives in rural areas, "operating a peasant economy" (1981, 150), where traditions are so cohesive that alien objects like books to be read in private are highly suspect, or at least so peculiar that they command everyone's nosy curiosity. In the rural environment, he argues, one's "individuality . . . is submerged in communality" (1981, 150). As a result, for the older generations, the few who read at all extensively did so "probably because they have been conditioned by their education to find time for quiet contemplation of literature that is spiritually and morally edifying." He guesses that it is among the younger generation, however – and this is in contrast to Griswold's predictions – where the habit might really take hold. Having "sought jobs in urban areas," they have finally "taken leave of . . . communal ties," and in "a relatively lonely environment, young people have substituted communion with books for relatives" (1981, 148). Urbanization is releasing "individuated experiences," he states – very much echoing the early sociology of Emile Durkheim and Georg Simmel. Reading is one of these experiences, Kotei argues, serving the needs of those in search of moral instruction and a feeling of togetherness with others.[1]

Though I would not endorse Kotei's derisive take on the "syndrome" of communalism, there is likely some truth to his argument about the affront to traditional sociality that reading presents. As people move into cities looking for work, whether or not they lose touch with their primary languages, they will often simply become immersed in English as the lingua franca of the urban hustle. This process has been rapid in recent years – we need only think again of the emergence of Lagos as a global megacity. Benanav notes that "between 1980 and the present, the world's waged workforce grew by about 75 per cent, adding more than 1.5 billion

---

[1] See for instance Durkheim's study (1893) of anomie as an urban condition of being too individualized, cut off from the norms of a supporting social whole; or see "The Metropolis and Mental Life" (1903), in which Simmel argues that city life allows the individual a complex and ambivalent freedom that manifests, especially in crowds, as loneliness.

Rural population (% of total population) – Nigeria

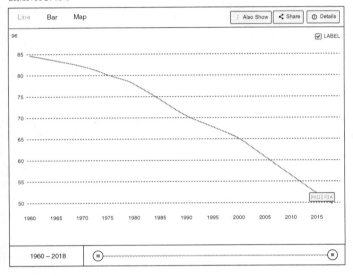

Figure 1 Rural population figures for Nigeria from 1960 to 2018. Chart created by the author using World Bank statistics.

people to the world's labour markets." Today "a much larger share of the world's population depends on finding work in labour markets in order to live" (2019, 37). This change has been dramatic in Africa. Just staying with the example of Nigeria, statistics gathered by the World Bank suggest that the current rural population is about 49.7 percent, steadily down from 84.59 percent in 1960, with no reason to expect any change in direction of population flows.

In light of this rapid transformation, we can observe that if the reading habit is currently spreading and changing, this is less because of the tireless work of charitable donors and developmentalist agencies actively trying to intervene, and more due to rapid urbanization and the immersion into English of people scrambling for work and daily livelihoods. It seems no longer quite right to say "the English-reading audience in countries such as Nigeria, Ghana and Kenya is restricted to those who can afford to pursue higher levels of education" such that "when discussing readership in anglophone African countries, one is actually referring to a small elite" (Lizzaríbar Buxó 1998, 24). This may apply well to the more literary readership, where longer and more dense materials are common for reading, and where texts are often more detached from functional uses and allocated their own special time as a tribute to their inherent value. But in the more demotic mass reading sector, where the sheer size of the potential reading population is quite considerable, we might guess that reading short texts on one's phone, including fiction, or ephemeral print picked up en route, even just to pass one's time during a boring day or commute, or to recuperate between work tasks, may become a growing daily habitual practice.

We observe then, alongside the slums and the rich gated suburbs, a persistent unevenness within the African English-language reading milieu itself, where we find small networks of reading as an elite pastime and cultural cultivation in a bifurcated system; we find schoolchildren exchanging sensationalistic supplementary readers produced in the informal sector; we find pressure to learn to read coupled with a lack of books at school; and we find demotic everyday reading of whatever comes your way, often speedy and ephemeral and haphazard and not easily statistically accounted for by me or any other interested observer. The fact of this other non-literary reading culture has long been observed, for instance in foundational scholarship on market literatures by Emmanuel Obiechina (1973), Stephanie Newell (2006), and Esther de Bruijn (2018). Scholars might now amplify and reanimate the claims of this work, by stressing the expansion of the audience for English texts that can be bought cheaply, shared readily, and read relatively quickly.

Hence my argument that what is not of much use here are the binary terms that usually feature in scholarship on literary publishing: mainstream versus alternative; large and corporate versus small and independent; commercial versus noncommercial or artistic. This vocabulary pits the mainstream against the independent, the corporate against the authentically literary. It emerged from study of what Pierre Bourdieu (1983) influentially called relatively "autonomous" literary fields, which were situated in advanced economies. In these fields, a considerable number of writers became able to making a living selling their books to an interested public, which then made it possible for some to toy with the idea that it bothered them when good art is tainted by commerce. Perhaps their work did not sell well but they had another source of income ("emancipation ... can be performed and pursued only if the post [of artist or poet] encounters the appropriate dispositions, such as disinterestedness and daring, and the (external) condition of these virtues, such as a private income" [Bourdieu 1983, 343]); perhaps they were willing to live in relative penury; or perhaps they were simply using anti-commercial posturing to sell more books. Whatever the case, we see many differences from the conditions Bourdieu considered when we look at the nature of English reading in the underdeveloped economies. For example, much of the activity in the high-literary field is funded not by market sales but by private foundation and nonprofit NGO investments. Furthermore, the relevant conundrum is not whether to "sell out" and go commercial, but rather how to acknowledge and manage one's dependence on foreign readers and outlets.

It is more useful to develop an alternative schema, mapping two separate but interlinked domains: on the one hand, developmentalist publishing; and on the other hand, the publishing picaresque. Developmentalist publishing has as its goal a more extensive legal industry with a wider predictable readership. It is supported by local writers who simultaneously depend on foreign audiences and want to develop local literary fields even though their work sells well abroad. It is also supported by funding from NGOs, foreign governments, private foundations, and the like. It works symbiotically with private-sector firms that want to cultivate audiences and sell more books. It imagines literacy and especially reading for improvement as a universal good. It laments underdevelopment of the sector. Picaresque publishing, on the other hand, is more about survival and entrepreneurialism in the moment. It is not really engaged in practices designed to expand official licensed publishing and book industries, but instead responds in a more immediate way to new kinds of needs for emergent forms of readily digestible reading materials.

Developmentalist publishing tends to cluster with Western-facing higher literary forms and with the paperbound book, though this last, the paperbound book, is perhaps an unsustainable and at least a residual relation. Picaresque publishing, on the other hand, tends more to serve local cash-strapped audiences; it is more aligned with demotic popular urbans forms, with piracy, and with reading materials that are not quite books as we have known them – with what we can describe as picaresque forms, then, like flash fiction and short uplifting poems read on smartphones. An irony, then, that there is no reason to believe that developmentalist publishing is a more effective inculcator of English-language literacy than the entrepreneurial picaresque. On the contrary.

3 How Europe Underdeveloped African Literature

How did the development industries, in all their NGO, nonprofit, and private foundation variants, become so crucial to publishing in Africa? The history of printing in English in Africa has been of interest to many scholars, who find that its early impetus was the missionary drive attending colonization. The Christian churches used the printed word to spread their religion in various languages, but especially English, and colonial governments followed suit. Affiliation with church teachings and with literacy in English promised social mobility. Even in more secular schools, education was – and continues to be – associated with moral teachings leading students onto the right path. Many people learned to read in English at school, while schooling and social mobility were clearly linked. (The commentators we encounter below, who bemoan the excessive moralism of African texts, seem to fail to recognize the ongoing power of these links.) It stands to reason that in a context in which reading happened mainly at school, and then became post-school a relatively indulgent expense, it needed to be used wisely. The observation that the majority of African readers have tended to be practically minded, preferring self-help, nonfiction, and religious texts to creative literature, and even reading fiction itself as guidance for life or useful training, is foundational to the whole field (Newell 2002, 3). One might consider again Wendy Griswold's pioneering ethnographic study of reading in Nigeria, where she finds that "reading is inclined to be more instrumental than ludic, more aimed at acquiring skills and knowledge needed for social and occupational mobility" (2000, 110).

The dominance of specifically English-language literacy is highly significant. There are at least 2,000 other languages spoken across Africa, but English became so exceptionally powerful for well-known reasons – because of the obvious kinds of capacity and capital that could be "obtained with its mastery," especially "economic and social mobility" (Lizzaríbar Buxó 1998, 9). In the former British colonies education became inseparable from literacy in English, and to a considerable extent reading itself has largely meant reading in English; as for the most part going to school meant learning English and becoming literate, and learning English meant finding a more secure economic footing in life. It has operated as a feedback loop. A hierarchy came to separate those with access and those without, with people slotted into the rankings based on the extent of their aptitude, measured for instance by the grace of their pronunciation, their ability to write grammatically, and the size of their vocabulary.

Consider here the interesting alliance between English and social aspiration even in a case like the Kenyan urban "peer languages" of Sheng and Engsh: Engsh, which derives structure and lexicon from English, is more characteristic of youth cultures in the wealthier parts of Nairobi, and signifies belonging to a wealthier subculture, whereas Sheng, which takes basic structure and lexicon from Swahili, is more characteristic of the city's less affluent and slum areas (Abdulaziz & Osinde 1997, 43). As Abiodun Goke-Pariola writes: "In a political economy where education was used, as has always been the case, as a means of acquiring the cultural capital necessary for certification for inclusion into the higher levels of the power structure, the principal medium of that rite was English" (1993, 139). Too often observers who position English print culture as a mark of modernity and social development, and who support the growth of the "reading habit" and the book industries, unthinkingly partake of the same situation that Goke-Pariola so carefully skewers: education equals English literacy equals relative cultural capital and relative social power.

Considering the history of these linkages is crucial to understanding the contemporary situation. The use of printing presses for colonial missionary work was backed by colonial governments. These governments played a further role in turn in the establishment of new school systems that needed textbooks. In the 1940s, 1950s, and 1960s foreign publishing houses including Oxford University Press, Macmillan, Heinemann, and Longman set up branches to provide these books for schools. However, they failed to do much of anything to develop local printing facilities. As local conditions were hardly promising – lacking even a reliable power grid, for instance – it was easier and cheaper to import books printed abroad. Thus the Kenyan publisher and scholar Henry Chakava writes wryly of Oxford University Press, which began operations in Nigeria in 1949 and in Kenya in 1954, that its aim was "to collect good manuscripts and forward them to London for vetting and publishing" (Chakava 2019, 203).

In nearly every country after independence there was some agitation to reform the education system away from European models, and there was in certain instances "an active involvement from some states to establish local printing presses under African control" (Lizzaríbar Buxó 1998, 37). Strict breakups were not practical, however. Instead foreign publishers negotiated new relationships to local governments, often appointing local directors and moving away from imported textbooks to use local printing facilities, often official government printers. These operations were still headquartered in the developed economies, however, and while degrees of local independence varied, there is little doubt that foreign firms remained dominant.

The small volume of publishing activity located within Africa itself has been a concern of development agencies since at least the 1950s. Writing as UNESCO's Director of Free Flow of Information and Book Development, Julian Behrstock notes that the book industry experts who met in Accra in 1968 "found that only six African countries produced books in national languages and that in some countries there is no publishing at all" (1975, 79). They estimate "book production amounted to only six titles per year for every million inhabitants and that no more than one-thirtieth of a book was available per person per year" (1975, 79). Those local books that did exist were mainly dry textbooks, unlikely to keep people from "relapsing into illiteracy" after they had finished school (1975, 79). With such statistics in mind, the African book industries became a target of significant interventions by UNESCO and others in the 1970s – a continuation of its sponsored research since the 1950s expressing concern about a "book hunger" in Africa. It made 1972 the International Year of the Book with many activities planned for Africa, in support of what local governments were already doing to try to develop local printing and publishing capacities.

These activities paid off somewhat, but not in a reliable way, and growth was hardly extraordinary. Chakava describes 1970 to 1977 as "a period of prosperity" for Kenyan publishing, but seven years are not very many, and the small gains made were not maintained – in fact they were lost (2019, 208). This was true generally. Kotei writes in his UNESCO-backed study that "it is undeniable that African publishing has made impressive strides: the number of titles published nearly doubled from 4,300 in 1965 to 8,300 in 1977; the number of titles per million inhabitants rose from eighteen to twenty-six in the same period" (1981, 5). Yet still, another expert observer points out, "Africa accounted for 1.1 percent of the number of titles published worldwide in 1955, but by 1975 the number had increased only to 1.9 percent and in 1977 it fell to 1.7 percent. For the world as a whole, the increase in book production between 1955 and 1977 was on the order of 43 percent" (Rathgeber 1985, 59).

Many aspiring local print publishers faced a shortage printing equipment, of computers and software, and of many basic materials. Nor could they count on a reliable supply of electricity or telephone and internet access. Already highly capitalized foreign companies, meanwhile, no longer had to jump over the same hurdles: "they [had] the capital, technology, expertise and infrastructure (for the purpose of distribution and marketing) which are sorely lacking at a local level" (Lizzaríbar Buxó 1998, 51). All of this tended to make local book industry infrastructure a poor investment. Local firms struggled to earn the trust of authors, who would hope that their books would be distributed widely and advertised well. While there are some reasonably successful regional alliances, industry insiders have continued to complain about inadequate distribution, especially between African nations, with prohibitive tariffs; and who has a budget for extensive marketing or the contacts to facilitate it? There has been an "absence of trained, qualified professionals within all sectors of the field, including managers, editors, booksellers, and librarians," and few courses available for those who might be interested (Lizzaríbar Buxó 1998, 62). No wonder then that writers who might want guarantees of "a higher quality product" have often turned their sights abroad when looking for publishers. It has been what Lizzaríbar Buxó calls a "vicious circle" – "a well-established mechanism which hinders the growth of an African book industry by continuously directing its resources and products towards an external supplier and consumer" (1998, 59).

Yet all the while, as these conditions have become sedimented, the international audience for African writing in English has been growing, and a canon of writing has become remarkably popular and well-regarded, not least through the intervention of Western firms working via branch locations in Africa. "The growth of African studies programs in North America and Europe, as well as the international recognition garnered by

African writers through prizes and awards, has ensured a strong international market for African books," Lizzaríbar Buxó writes (1998, 49). Cultivation of the market via high-profile projects like the Heinemann African Writers Series (AWS) was an important catalyst here – a good example of a hybrid endeavor blending local involvement and foreign production. The AWS was sketched out by Heinemann Educational Books directors Van Milne and Alan Hill in the late 1950s, "when rapidly approaching African independence and anticipated educational advances suggested new opportunities" (Griswold 2000, 62). As Griswold puts it, they saw "supply and demanding converging: a generation of writers educated after WWII, often at the new African universities, coincided with the educational ambitions and cultural aspirations of the new nations" (2000, 62).

The series launched in 1962, putting out relatively affordable paperbacks for use by students. Chinua Achebe was appointed the first advisory editor, and he stayed in that role into 1972. The series published Achebe, Wole Soyinka, Ngũgĩ wa Thiong'o and others – a who's who, really, of African literature in English. These titles were sold to African schools as supplementary readers for English classes, as well as to university students in Africa and to readers abroad. However, much of the marketing and editorial work happened in London, and nor were the books printed locally. Their existence very much mattered to people who aspired to write and wanted to read books by African writers, yet their production did little to change the economic conditions that determined the general situation on the ground for publishers, printers, distributors, and sellers of printed objects in Africa.

Similar observations can be made about Oxford University Press's Three Crowns series (1962–1976), which played an important role in producing and disseminating African literature when it was first gaining a foothold in Western markets. Caroline Davis's research (2013) on the way in which Three Crowns served lucrative African schoolbook markets by appealing to Oxford's foreign academic prestige is crucial here. Oxford University Press secured its vast cultural capital by highlighting its non-commercial investments in brands like Clarendon Press, and by publishing academic titles selected for largely white non-African academic markets. Yet it was the funds gained through extensive sales of educational material in the African market that bankrolled its more academic and noncommercial ventures. Its production of texts for African schoolchildren was only minimally an African affair. When specific editors and managers did hire Africans to work in the branch offices, this most often occurred under pressure from official indigenization policies. Meanwhile attempts to wrest actual editorial power away from London would fail. The local branch offices were permitted to acquire works to circulate in the local school markets but were advised to send manuscripts to London for potential inclusion in the Three Crowns series first. The Three Crowns series took works deemed to be of the right level of aesthetic sophistication, while inferior products were left for the branch offices to publish for school use where appropriate, often as supplementary readers to accompany standard curricula. The result of this marked asymmetry was, undoubtedly, the perpetuation of what Davis describes as colonial structures of literary production and distribution.

The cases of Heinemann's AWS and Oxford University Press's Three Crowns series suggest the crucial role that British publishers played in establishing the canon of emerging African literature. Writers who were judged worthy of inclusion in these prestigious series could pass through them and from there on into the general British trade press, once they were deemed to have attracted a sufficient measure of international acclaim. The general trade press lists were still the top of the ladder of success; the educational markets managed by local branch offices and supplied with supplementary readers were lower down. The official book series were mediating middle rungs. They were edited and controlled in part from esteemed overseas firms, and profits and salaries were concentrated there as well. In turn, while a market for African literature was cultivated overseas, it was in part funded by sales to African schools that were modeled on European public education systems. These required supplementary primers to help students master English, arguably throwing those students yet further into a situation of neocolonial dependency. Projects like AWS and Three Crowns were marketed as a boon to African readers, and to be sure in some respects they were. But they did not escape the logic of expropriation of profits, of marshaling of resources in favor of English as the dominant language, and of concentrating gatekeepers and gatekeeping institutions in colonial centers. In fact, in the 1970s Oxford University

Press's Ibadan branch was hardly some dusty peripheral outpost, it was instead its most profitable branch. In 1977, its "turnover peaked at £9 million, representing over 20 per cent of Oxford University Press's total turnover of £46 million" (Davis 2013, 44–45). In this real way, sales of books for learning readers in Africa backed the rest of the Oxford University Press publishing program, allowing it to publish things like low-selling monographs by white European academics.

In sum, research on English-language publishing in Africa has emphasized that the formal publishing and book industries are relatively underdeveloped because of the low rates of literacy and high rates of poverty; with fewer readers to buy titles, publishers do not have incentive to take risks or expand; foreign firms from the wealthy former colonizing nations have had the unfair advantage of capital from the head corporation, which effectively stymies indigenous development. There are additional factors that could be mentioned here, such as foreign charitable book donation schemes, which arguably further inhibit local development (see Smith 1977), and – to be discussed further in Section 6 – a rampant culture of book plagiarism and piracy, which threatens profits for legally established firms. Of course, the very existence of a threat from book pirates suggests that, at least in the "submerged but vibrant" informal sector (Newell 2002, 2), potential readers and materials for printing may not be especially scarce.

It is often lamented that African governments do not invest in the things that would make higher forms of reading more accessible or appealing – such as library development, book prizes, or funding for writers. In fact, they have invested in these things decreasingly since the 1970s, when global economic crises and World Bank and International Monetary Fund (IMF) structural adjustment programs began to ramify in ways that basically decimated their already weakened public spending capacities. They have, understandably, other priorities. If states have relatively meager tax bases from which to draw funds for social programming, this is due to a combination of factors such as Britain's expropriation of wealth during the colonial period, dramatic lack of investment in postcolonial public institutions and structures of governance, the ongoing stripping of resources by foreign companies, and dramatically low rates of formal employment. We do not often think about the relationship between the size of a local literary field and the extent of absorption of labor into the "legitimate" workforce – that is, state regulated and taxable labor – but this relationship is very real, and being aware of it helps us to understand the real causes of Africa's "book poverty."

Though not often expressly interested in this sort of critique of postcolonial political economy, scholars of African literature have certainly noted that publishing industry conditions matter to what and how people read. At the "low" end, with the various relatively ephemeral market literatures, for example, scholars have observed that readers are conscious of what economists refer to as transactional utility. They are reluctant to spend time and money on things unless they serve a practical purpose, such as supplementing school curricula or promising moral uplift. Once people are out of school, this reluctance deepens. Leisure, solitude, quiet, and extra money are scarce resources. Meanwhile in the more elite milieu, it would seem to be relatively straight path from the small scale of local book production in Africa to dependence on metropolitan centers for cultivation and circulation of African literatures. African literary production has been read through the "educationally reinforced dependency-mechanisms by which many African writers and, by corollary, their local readers are persuaded to believe that cultural value, as well as economic power, is located and arbitrated elsewhere" (Huggan 2019, 210). It has been understood as necessarily therefore "extroverted" (Julien 2006) – that is, appealing or even pandering to a Western readership – or as "self-anthropologizing" (Ede 2015), that is, willingly and self-consciously putting itself forward as a form of education and insight into an unfamiliar other culture.

While my focus here is English-language publishing, it is worthwhile to compare it briefly to the situation of local non-English African-language publishing. It is fairly clear that the challenges posed to those wanting to expand publishing in local languages are even more crushing – amongst them, as in the case of English-language publishing, undercapitalization, the absence of buyers, the paucity of state support for things like library acquisitions, and the clear presence of nonprofit charities stepping into the breach to provide free or cheap materials through supported programs. Additional challenges for local language publishing encompass the costs associated with language development, including "special typography for tonal differences in non-standardised scripts" (Zell 2018, 5), and the fact that so many families continue to prefer their children learn and use English.

As Ngũgĩ stated in a recent interview:

> those that write in African languages remain invisible, their works are hardly ever reviewed or translated. Publishing venues are limited and getting published is one of the most infuriating challenges of writing in African languages. There are hardly any publishing houses devoted to African languages. So writers in African languages are writing against great odds: no publishing houses, no state support, and with national and international forces aligned against them. Prizes are often given to promote African literature but on the condition that the writers don't write in African languages. (Dyssou 2017)

Ngũgĩ's own case is telling in this respect. He famously broke with the English language, beginning his book, *Decolonising the Mind*, with the now famous declaration that "This book . . . is my farewell to English as a vehicle for any of my writings. From now on it is Gĩkũyũ and Kiswahili all the way" (1986, xiv). Yet we need only read as far as the next sentence before we reach his important caveat: "However, my hope is that through the age-old medium of translation I shall be able to continue dialogue with all" – recognizing, therein, that to write only in Gĩkũyũ or Kiswahili, and not be translated into English, would be in one scholar's phrase "tantamount to undertaking an adventure in obscurity" (Owoeye & Dada 2015, 108). Ngũgĩ thus opts not so much to leave English completely behind but rather to build into his authorial technique a constant reminder of the status of the colonizing language. He does this precisely because it is such a challenge to build a sustainable career as a writer in non-English African languages, given what has been described as their "low status, marginalisation and exclusion of indigenous languages in post-independent African media systems" versus "the hegemonic influence of ex-colonial languages" (Mpofu & Salawu 2018, 293).

Hans Zell notes that while more than 2,000 living languages are spoken in Africa, amounting to something like 30 percent of the world's total living languages, most have zero or a miniscule publishing culture (2018, 3). He argues that:

> In most African countries public library services or national library boards have traditionally been the biggest purchasers of African language titles in the past, usually buying in bulk quantities. However, many library services now operate with pitiful book buying budgets, or new acquisitions have ceased altogether. Instead, government officials and policy makers in Africa would appear to view book donations from abroad as the most effective and most economical method of providing books to their libraries, at no cost to them. For public libraries they do not seem to see a need to provide them with book acquisitions budgets. (2018, 6)

These remarks are telling in the way they echo the refrain – we will see it again soon – that basically castigates local governments for failures to provide people with quality books, an essential good. Zell adheres here to the taken-for-granted common sense associations between reading and human development.[2] He shows little sign of interest in any underlying causes that make it difficult for African states to invest money in expanding

---

[2] Compare also Henry Chakava writing in 2008, at a time of serious pessimism about the possibility of global economic development:

> African book development is part and parcel of African development itself, and cannot be seen in isolation. The book does not reside where there is extensive poverty, where people have no access to medical care; where there is inadequate shelter and poor roads, where there is no food. The book thrives where there is a responsive government that provides security, good governance, shies away from graft, and constructively engages its citizenry in nation building – in such an environment it will be possible to develop strategies that can enable government and industry to marshal the resources and manpower needed to take African book development to the next stage. (2008, x)

readership. Instead he seems to assume that people should acquire middle-class habits despite living in places that lack the fundamental grounds for these habits – grounds such as low unemployment and governments with capacity for fulsome social spending. Zell even suggests that states are taking advantage of charity, preferring a handout to the hard work of self-development, as it were. Yet surely book donation schemes simply partake of a broader dependence on nonprofits and NGOs for provision of goods, in a situation in which remunerative employment is not easy to come by, especially in the legal sector, so people must find other ways to survive despite not having waged work?

The situation is slightly less dire in South Africa for local language publishers, but even there it seems that commercial presses will publish in non-English African languages if there are government policies – and so commercial incentives – that support learning these languages for reasons of cultural uplift and preservation. While a culturalist or nationalist argument for support for local language publishing may make it easier to get going, it is in the nature of such programs to be short-lived. In their work on South Africa's government-sponsored Indigenous Language Publishing Programme (ILPP), Jana Möller and Beth le Roux (2017) discuss the reluctance and incapacity of the Department of Arts and Culture to fund the project on a permanent basis. The picture that thus emerges is of a local language press dependent on temporary and sometimes niche culturalist sentiment and precarious funding from states with shifting priorities.

As it happens, government neglect of the needs of a cultivated literary sphere – or its at best haphazard and unreliable commitments – has become quite fundamental to how some literary practitioners and their supporters envision their own work today. Some now identify as "literary activists," arguing that, given the real barriers faced by those who want to work in and expand the literary field in Africa, supporting the African literary economy via engagement with small enterprises is itself a kind of activism. In a forthcoming article, Madhu Krishnan and Kate Wallis discuss this activist understanding of work within the African literary milieu, arguing that emerging literary networks are interesting because they "defy an easy categorization under the terms of both the capitalist, global literary market and what we might simplistically refer to as resistance to the same." If I may paraphrase their treatment: in contemporary African conditions, there is nothing compromising about trying to expand the market. Instead the work of encouraging market growth is itself politically progressive in a meaningful way. Given state neglect, who has the luxury of being offended by commerce?

Krishnan and Wallis cite a speech by Bwesigye bwa Mwesigire, founder of Arts Managers and Literary Activists (AMLA), in which he describes literary activism as a direct response to the absence of African government support for literary activity:

> we use the word activism because as you realize the African literary and cultural scene is not supported by governments. It is not a problematic generalization to say that most African countries took to neoliberal free market policies so there is no government funding for the arts. [...] It's activism to actually have spaces for which artists can create.

Forgive me for wondering once more at the idea that African states are relatively poor because of their embrace of neoliberalism. As I have asked above, how much choice did they have given the global neoliberal drift and IMF and World Bank imposed structural adjustment programs? How small are their social spending budgets given dramatic expropriation and non-investment by the former colonial powers, and current un- and under-employment with so little income tax predictably collected? What Walter Rodney wrote in 1972 remains germane today:

> If independent Africa is still without the benefits of modern education, as it is, the seventy-five years of colonial exploitation undoubtedly have something to do with the state of affairs; and the absurdity is so much the greater when one contemplates how much Africa produced in that period and how much of that went to develop all aspects of European capitalist society, including its educational institutions. (1972, 246)

The underdevelopment of social spending capacity in African states has a profound impact on the nature of the local literary field. Indeed, one could very well speak of how Europe underdeveloped African literature.

In any case, it is in thinking about systemic underdevelopment that we begin to understand the shadow of neglect that literary activists aim to address as they seek funding support from other sources, including foreign governments and private foundations. Of course, the aim of literary activists is less a critique of neocolonial political economy than it is a real-world intervention in on-the-ground activity within the literary milieu, justified by a high estimation of literary culture as such. In the next two sections, I look more closely at how the high-literary milieu that does exist has been shaped by the general absence of local supports described thus far.

4 "Nuance," or: The Contemporary High-Literary Scene

Moving into the more contemporary period, we can continue to observe the considerable forces inhibiting the development of anything like large well-capitalized book industries in Africa, and can attend to the realities of unevenness as they structure the cultivation of reading. Thinking about the high-literary as a category, we can emphasize once more, echoing Griswold, some conditions that need to be in place for cultivation of what we would readily recognize as a high-literary sensibility.[3] These conditions include a certain level of education, belief in the value of literary reading, reliable light, quiet uninterrupted time, and a place to sit in relative solitude. When we highlight these conditions, we can see that the literary has tended to be one expression of a kind of dominance, or one concretization of the "upward" toward which people are supposed to want to be "mobile." Dominance inheres in things like the aura of the "quality" paperback, the nature of the physical appearance of that slightly larger "B" format book printed on good paper, with a sturdy binding and usually quite sedate non-salacious cover art. African writing in this category – the high-literary niche – remains a relatively exclusive practice.

There is an important African literary community currently thriving across key cities. They are a coterie, often working with donor support for their publications and workshops, and able to build upon the connections and synergies that exist within any small, relatively wealthy group of cultural producers and consumers – journalists, musicians, academics, and so on. Writers who belong to this particular coterie are published abroad, supported by US creative writing programs and English department professorships, and by US- and UK-based literary agencies, especially Andrew Wylie's agency, which represents so many of the best known African writers, including Chimamanda Adichie, NoViolet Bulawayo, Teju Cole,

---

[3] See also Richard Altick's classic study *The English Common Reader*, which argues that the "domestic hurly-burly" of one's homelife, living in close and noisy quarters, as well as fatigue and lack of light, made reading very difficult for working people in nineteenth-century London, and influenced what they did read when they could (1957, 91–93).

and Taiye Selasi. As a result, while there is a small readership in these urban centers, it is simply not that important that there be massive numbers of local readers. These writers have bypassed the problem of the absent African reader. There is donor funding to support the activity of African writing, to award prizes to African authors, and to facilitate these authors' access to US and other foreign markets.

A key node in the network is Kwani Trust, a Kenya-based literary network that emerged from an email conversation among writers and interconnected cultural luminaries, and which is funded by the US-based Ford Foundation. It was founded in 2003, when Binyavanga Wainaina, who won the 2002 Caine Prize for African Writing, returned to Kenya after ten years as a student and journalist in South Africa. A group started to meet in person in Nairobi – what soon became regular garden parties – and they decided it would be a good idea to start a new publishing house to publish African writers in Kenya. It also launched online the literary journal *Kwani?* with Wainaina as its first editor, and secured its funding; in its early years, Kwani Trust received between 100,000 and 255,000 USD yearly from the Ford Foundation. These amounts have increased alongside the Trust's output: in 2009 it was 395,000 USD; in 2011 it was 600,000 USD.

Doreen Strauhs has studied Kwani Trust as a primary example of a new phenomenon of specifically literary NGOs which offer what she describes as a distinct model for African writing in English. These "LINGOs" – Literary NGOs – support literary talent, events, and publishing in the nonprofit sector; they are registered as nonprofits, or for tax purposes separate for-profit from nonprofit activities and grants from earned income. They depend on international funding and are independent of local governments. Kwani Trust was registered as a trust in 2003 precisely because it was the "quickest legal body to form . . . to allow for the absorption of grants and donations" (2013, 12).

Why is the Ford Foundation so invested in funding African literary organizations? This is difficult to answer. Their own declarations about their programs tend to be overly general, with more buzzwords than concrete program descriptions. A 2007 press release mentions a desire to support "efforts to secure the safety and well-being of citizens; expand democratization and civic participation; strengthen the capacity of local philanthropies and non-profits; advance creativity in the arts; strengthen freedom of expression and celebrate diversity in heritage and identity; and build new partnerships for peace and social justice" (Ford Foundation 2007). This is quite a mandate.

One way to begin to parse it is by considering a recent controversy, when the Ford Foundation came under scrutiny after current president Darren Walker posted a piece on the organization's homepage, titled "In Defense of Nuance." Pitched as a response to a hardening of positions he had witnessed in policy debates, Walker's piece laments that people do not try to build bridges anymore, instead actively sacrificing "relationships based on mutual understanding" (Walker 2019). They settle into an "oppositional, nuance-averse posture" which insists on "ideological purity and public shame" (Walker 2019). Included in his defense of nuance is the clue to his real motivation, which is to undermine radical prison abolitionists. Walker has been closely involved in efforts to decide the fate of the prison population after the impending closure of the Rikers Island complex, and so insists here on measured discussion of prison reform – advocating for example not the abolition of prison but rather "hold[ing] new jails to account" for human rights violations, while trying to "address the root causes of mass incarceration." "We cannot let the perfect be the enemy of progress," he counsels; instead a nuanced, reform-minded, bridge-building approach is required (Walker 2019).

Critics of the piece pointed out that Warren's argument jived well with the historic pacifying role of the Ford Foundation in the US public sphere. Some of its core activities have been "in funding and shaping the institutionalization of African American Studies" in ways designed to "neutralize Black and "Third World" student protest" and marginalize more radical scholars (Rodríguez 2019). In Dylan Rodríguez's terms, the Ford Foundation's "periodic piecemeal reforms of racist state policing, criminological, and carceral practices, and hundreds of successful local, statewide, and national electoral campaigns for public office" have "contributed to a *disciplining* of political imaginaries that facilitates rather than resisting and opposing the institutional and cultural logics of White Reconstruction" (Rodríguez 2019) – logics that include mass and disproportionate imprisonment of black people. Other scholars have similarly observed that it was during an era of intense instability in urban centers in the late 1960s that the Ford Foundation stepped up its interventions in order to quell disquiet and ease social tensions, not least through the funding of particular kinds of black cultural production. Karen Ferguson argues for example (2013) that as prospects for impoverished black people in inner cities deteriorated, the Ford Foundation further emphasized elite high-art development and individual upward mobility, including backing the Black Arts movement and the development of Black Studies programs at universities.

The language the Ford Foundation uses to describe its recent work in Africa suggests some immediate parallels with its history in the United States. Current program descriptions claim that the organization has been motivated to "to support the region's transition to democracy through the 1980s and 1990s, assisting in its progression to a more democratic environment through reforms of laws, state institutions, and economic policies." They state that their focus since 2000 has been on the "well-being of citizens" and equipping people "to participate in the expansion of democracy" (Ford Foundation 2020). It is about "acting as engaged citizens"; warding off the threat of ethnic violence by "advancing democracy, fairness, opportunity, and human rights"; building "renewed assets and trust among communities" (Ford Foundation 2020). A few key words and phrases appear time and again: citizen; democracy; justice; human rights; institution building.

Grants to art and cultural organization have been a part of this same work. According to official program statements, art and culture helps "strengthen cultural identity and understanding as well as free expression" (Ford Foundation 2020). Funded literary organizations are expected to contribute to an informed, empowered, civil society. They should celebrate the free expression of artists untrammeled by state repression and offer training for participation in the public sphere by teaching writing and communication networking. The Ford Foundation basically empowers local grantees to develop programs to foster an elite sphere of political discussion and cultural expression. Their funding is a boon to the success of a small cultural sector that has a significant voice and access to the means of amplification. Just for example, they adhere to a vision of liberal capitalist democracy that positions things like undemocratic elections and ethnic conflict as the key threats – rather than, say, underlying global phenomena such as environmental degradation and the search for work driving people into cities. We can say then in sum, that the point of the Ford Foundation's cultural funding in Africa is to help to prop up the legitimacy of development toward capitalist market dominance, by amplifying voices that are against radical social transformation.

At this point my analysis may seem a long way from a consideration of English reading in Africa, but I maintain that the connections between literary phenomena and underlying institutional supports with their own ideological tendencies are far more pressing and relevant than we tend to think. After all, the Ford Foundation is only one of the players here. Similar observations could made about the Rockefeller Foundation, which traditionally funded African literature and university departments in its efforts to advance US foreign policy interests – "to create a new African "elite" whose embrace of free market economics would gradually trickle down," as one critic puts it (Eatough 2019, 137) – and which now supports writers from Africa and elsewhere with residencies at its Bellagio Centre; or the Oppenheimer Memorial Trust, funded by the wealth that Ernest Oppenheimer acquired through diamond and gold mining, which funds the Caine Prize for African Writing. This is not one philanthropist's special passion. It is a massive donor complex. The funding of African literary organizations by these private foundations is part and parcel of a broader effort to empower particular civic actors and thus particular ways of thinking and talking – a conversation amongst people of relative wealth and status, committed to an ostensible political neutrality in art and to a "civil" discussion. "Nuance," if you will. The literary milieu is being cultivated as one wing of a whole field of empowered political and cultural actors who set the terms of what counts as a civil discussion, rational debate, and acceptable speech. The dominant effect is, as many have observed of the US scene, a neutralizing of more radical points of view, and so a covering over of other realities and ways of thinking.

My point is that this funding matrix is not incidental. Rather, it is key to what is happening in contemporary African literary culture today, where private foundation funding is so essential. The African writing emerging today would not exist in the same way without it. These foundations have

taken up the role of the old British publishing firms in fostering development of particular clusters of literary activities and values, with backing
from institutions of elite education in English. The private foundations fund
writing fellowships and workshops, and link to the elite schools and creative
writing programs, just as, for an earlier generation, a particular kind of
schooling was integral to one's positioning within the literary milieu – via
places like Government College Umuahia, for instance, described by Terri
Ochiagha as "the colonial equivalent of the British public school system
[that] proposed transformation of talented African youth into intellectually
empowered, yet powerfully quiescent colonial replicas of English gentle-
men" (2015, 9). She calls this education system "a political device, instilling
English cultural and political allegiance and the self-assurance of the chosen
College elite" (2015, 11). The parallels with private foundation funding in
the contemporary period should not be overlooked.

Interestingly, Strauhs notes that Kwani Trust writers consistently insist
that they work autonomously, neutrally, without political bias and inde-
pendently of any funding source; they "consider themselves as independent
write-tanks" (2013, 14). Kwani Trust operates at arm's length from the Ford
Foundation, and from the donor-funded Caine Prize, though there are clear
connections of friendship and influence between Ford personnel, Caine
judges and staff, and people involved with Kwani Trust. Many of the short
stories that have won the Caine Prize or have been shortlisted were
published in *Kwani?* and there has been speculation about Wainaina's
friendship with Nick Elam, a Caine Prize administrator. By Elam's own
account, while he knew the manager at the Ford Foundation in Kenya when
Kwani Trust received funding, this was not a factor in support for the
venture. It is not as though the Caine Prize set out to start a literary journal,
though that is how some people see it.

Kwani Trust does not understand itself as being involved in a situation
of dependency on charitable organizations. Instead they are simply business partners. All the buzzwords apply: partnerships, cultural entrepreneurship, creative economies, making flexible careers. These are all key
terms of Ford Foundation and related private donor activities across
Africa, as well as in intergovernmental initiatives such as UNESCO's
supports for cultural development. That writers see their work as separate

from any donor prerogative is symptomatic of the particular literary mentality that the Ford Foundation recognizes and supports – one of Strauhs' interviewees calls this "a *Kwani?* sensibility" (2013, 17). Strauhs observes that as a group Kwani Trust-affiliated writers agree that it is neither their job nor duty to fight for social and political change; they hate being pigeonholed in any way; they are not interested in debates, which they consider passé, about the politics of writing in English; they prefer to be transnational rather than tied to a particular African nation or identity (and indeed several, including Wainaina before he died, work in US English departments); and they are eager to emphasize their autonomy both from the Ford Foundation and from Kwani Trust. When Wainaina was named Young Global Leader by the World Economic Forum in 2006 – an award designed to recognize "potential to contribute to shaping the future of the world" – he turned the prize down. Reflecting on his decision later, he said it "would be an act of great fraudulence for me to accept the trite idea that I am 'going to significantly impact world affairs'" (quoted in Strauhs 2013, 19).

Kwani Trust's ties with other African organizations are crucial here as well. Kate Wallis's essential chronicling of the networks of African literary prestige (2018) provides many fascinating details. Mentioning just a few of the events and synergies she details will be enough. In Lagos early in 2010, A. Igoni Barrett, who had been an editor for *Farafina* magazine, launched an event called Book Jam at an upscale shopping mall on Victoria Island. His initial goal in starting the event series was the wish to sell more copies of his own short story collection *From Caves of Rotten Teeth*. At one event, Wainaina encountered Barrett's writing, and later, as Director of the Chinua Achebe Center at Bard College in the US, offered Barrett a writing fellowship. Barrett was thus able to complete a new manuscript, which Wainaina forwarded to his own agent, Sarah Chalfant, at the Wylie Agency. Wylie agreed to represent him, and soon Barrett had two books under contract. They were published in the US by what is perhaps *the* pivotal nonprofit independent publisher, Graywolf Press, and in the UK by Chatto & Windus, an imprint owned by Penguin Random House. Barrett also secured a writing residency at the Rockefeller Foundation's Bellagio Center.

Wainaina and Adichie have been premier cultural brokers, facilitating other writers' access to the mechanisms of publication and promotion. They have appeared at events promoting new works, such as Farafina's launch of Eghosa Imasuen's *Fine Boys*, which took place in 2012 at a bookstore in an affluent area of Lagos. Farafina is Adichie's long-time publisher in Nigeria, but the relationship goes much deeper than that. In 2007 Adichie launched what has become the annual Farafina Trust Creative Writing Workshop. Wainaina was himself in Lagos in 2012, and participated in the *Fine Boys* launch, because he was teaching with Adichie at the Farafina Trust Creative Writing Workshop, as he had been doing since 2007. An early version of the opening chapter of *Fine Boys* was published in *Kwani?* in 2010. Barrett not only worked at Farafina; it is his publisher in Nigeria. Barrett's novel *Blackass* was commissioned by Eghosa Imasuen, who in 2013 became Chief Operating Officer of Kachifo Limited, which owns the Farafina imprint; Imasuen has co-taught the Farafina Trust Creative Writing Workshop with Adichie and Wainaina. Wallis's detailed research (2018) proliferates examples like these.

Kwani? issues repeatedly draw from a small group of writers – which makes sense, one supposes, since their goal is "identifying and nurturing writers with potential" and engaging with their work in a sustained way. In issues 1 through 5, 103 authors were published, but there was a concentration of instances of publication within a small group, especially staff of the trust or journal, associated volunteers, and founding members (Strauhs 2013, 21). Furthermore, during the tenth anniversary celebrations, Kwani Trust's literary prize for unpublished manuscripts was given out by judge Ellah Wakatama Allfrey. Allfrey, who was born in Zimbabwe, is former Deputy Editor of *Granta*, has been a judge for the Man Booker Prize, and is Deputy Chair of the Council of the Caine Prize. Wallis also mentions Muthoni Garland, who was involved in the beginnings of Kwani Trust and has frequently been published in *Kwani?* In 2007 Garland started Storymoja with a group of other writers; it publishes more popular works and children's books, and for six years collaborated with the English Hay Festival to run the Storymoja Festival.

While it is fair to claim that the writing that emerges from this scene is Western-facing – targeted primarily at British and American markets – one could make the point with greater precision. The situation is one of donor-supported funding of networks of writers who are more dependent on each other as cultural brokers, on international donors, and on foreign markets, than they are on the existence of a local readership for literary works. Kwani Trust print publications are sold in bookshops, convenience stores, and supermarkets – mainly in Nairobi but also in select shops elsewhere. The key UK-based distributor of African books, the African Books Collective, is currently selling issues of *Kwani?* at prices that range between £19 and £30. In her study Strauhs notes local shops selling *Kwani?* for 23 USD and Kwaninis titles – which is a spinoff pocketsize series – for 10 USD. She wagers that this is too steep for the majority of Kenyans, where, the UN reports, the average daily earnings work out to about 4 USD, and most people live below the poverty line. As Strauhs points out – and at the risk of stating the obvious – the people involved in the trust's advancement possess "habitus, economic situation, and social status" that are "dramatically different from the majority of the Kenyan population" (2013, 24).

One cannot overlook here another crucial site for cultivation of a relatively elite literary sphere that is tasked with representing, and furthering, broader social and economic uplift: the writers' festival. Writers' festivals have grown phenomenally in recent years, from established players like the Zimbabwe International Book Fair, to newer hipper events like Storymoja, which has partnered with the Hay Festival, one of the biggest festival programmers in the world. One notable annual event is Writivism – the name itself linking writing automatically to activism. Writivism is a Ugandan festival curated by the Center for African Cultural Excellence (CACE), which was cofounded by Bwesigye bwa Mwesigire, one of the self-styled "literary activists" cited above. The list of program and funding partners for the most recent year is suggestive (Figure 2). I can spotlight just a few. Bakwa is a successful Cameroon-based literary and cultural magazine and publisher, which also produces a podcast and reading series. The Miles Morland Foundation was set up in 2013 by Miles Morland, a UK-based investor whose two companies, Blakeney Management and Development Partners International, invested in African development projects from real estate to stock market infrastructure. Like many philanthropists, he welcomes the tax breaks that result from charitable

Program Partners

Figure 2 Recent Writivism program partners. Shared with kind permission granted by organizer Bwesigye bwa Mwesigire.

giving as his dividends role in, and he funds things that soften the brand images attached to his corporate firms. The British Council is the British state's signature cultural diplomacy outfit, arranging distribution of suitable cultural fare across the globe since 1934.

In general, the culture of writers' festivals is tied tightly to urban planning mandates around support for visitor economies. They can be marketed as a form of cultivation of a general knowledge economy, in which a thriving literary scene and heritage are accoutrements that a cultured city can boast. Festivals promise new kinds of literary and cultural experiences that might incorporate new audiences. They are attractive to creative-industry boosters competing to encourage people to spend money in their cities, and they suit an audience that wants to have a literary experience that does not entail reading a long book. Hence, while university-based literary study and conventional print-based literary publishing may be struggling to stay afloat here and elsewhere, the value to be extracted from an idealized literary heritage persists, supported by the expanding literary festival circuit, the growth of culture-based tourism, and the branding and safeguarding of places and monuments associated with literary tradition. Festivals are in a sense among the various and dynamic new lives of literary culture, which have stepped in where other sites of reproduction of literature's value have diminished or disappeared.

Writers' festivals are often industry oriented, and so foster respect for creativity and intellectual property rights – panels on how copyright works are not infrequent – and the development of creative economies through networking and skills sharing with likeminded organizations. There is often, as there is here, funding from private foundations and from foreign cultural agencies. They host established writers, but also hold workshops for aspiring writers, other industry-orientated events about how to expand market share, and related cultural events such as art displays, film screenings, and intellectual debates. The marquee figures are often those top African writers who are about to sell well abroad – living off their literary careers and sometimes also working in permanent creative writing positions in universities. Literature festivals are, lastly, marketed to partners and to the public as alternatives to popular media – spaces where we can look to gifted learned people, to lettered thinkers, for guidance in troubled times, when unthinking rhetoric is all too rampant and "post-truth" rules the airwaves, and as a space for creative professionals to come together in sympathetic accord.

In all of these ways, they are really a summation of everything I have been wanting to refer to as the official developmentalist high-literary matrix: they involve scholars who are interested in the state of publishing in Africa; industry professionals and consultants (and these categories are not self-enclosed of course; scholars are increasingly consultants and so on);

famous writers who do not really need local audiences but are working to help other writers make careers; and philanthropists and NGO employees and others in the development field working toward economic and social development goals. They are all, big and small, invested in development of the publishing industry, expansion of readership and sales; and they are fairly uniformly invested in that familiar ideology of the book as a tool of enlightenment, whether this means, for some visitors, possession of books and affiliation with book culture as signs of election to superior humanity, or whether it means, say for workshop participants, the hope that they are honing a skill through which they may earn some money.

5 To "Nurse Ambition"

One final crucial dimension of this cultivated literary matrix, neglected thus far, is the English-language creative writing workshop. These have proliferated in a handful of African cities since about the mid-2000s, in a context in which university creative writing seminars and Master of Fine Arts programs are rare, with those that do exist concentrated in a few places, especially South Africa. These workshops are often connected to the university sector, but they are not run by departments. Instead they are branches of the literary nonprofit organizations that have come to drive much of the high-literary scene in Africa. They are fairly unique to the African scene, where they serve as crucial links – pipelines, really – to publications and prizes. The urban literary nonprofits have what Doseline Kiguru describes as the accumulated cultural capital "necessary to link writers to prize organisations and publishers, and therefore to global visibility" (2016, 209). In turn most of the organizations in question, including Farafina Trust, Writivism, Storymoja, Kwani Trust and FEMRITE, host workshops as part of their mandate, targeting writers, editors, and publishers variously; and it is the workshops that are the key conduits for those seeking "access to major award organisations and international publishers" (Kiguru 2016, 205). In Kiguru's terms, "writers canonised by the international prize organisations have been sourced from these writers' organisations and in turn, these writers have used the economic and symbolic power achieved from the literary prizes to support local literary production through investments in writers' organisations, publications, as well as through creative writing workshops" (2016, 212). What this points to is how the ways into the field are relatively few; access to the top workshops and to the star figures who liaise with the workshops is clearly key.

I have highlighted already the example of the Caine Prize for African Writers Workshop established in 2003, which is funded by the Oppenheimer Memorial Trust. Participants' work is all but guaranteed publication and consideration for the Caine Prize. Workshop leaders are established figures with considerable industry connections. The writers invited to the workshop are specifically instructed to write a short story.

These are published in a Caine Prize anthology, alongside the stories shortlisted for the prize that year. They are also then submitted for consideration in the next year's Caine Prize competition. Another example is the Storymoja writers' workshops in Nairobi, which are held annually during the popular Storymoja Festival, and also continue on throughout the year in various guises. They are led by Storymoja's founding member, Muthoni Garland, with backing from Storymoja's various funders, including in recent years the British Council, the Hay Festival, the Caine Prize, the Miles Morland Foundation, HIVOS, and Book Aid International.

And there is Farafina Trust, also mentioned above – an interesting case of an organization which would seem to meet criteria for local Nigerian authenticity, and yet it is funded nearly entirely by Nigerian Breweries Plc, a subsidiary of the Heineken Group, one of the global giants in the alcohol industry. Farafina's aim is to promote contemporary African writing and reading. In addition to its well-liked magazine, it has put on a popular and competitive annual creative writing workshop whose facilitators have included some of the biggest names in African writing, including Chimamanda Ngozi Adichie, who has been more central to the creative writing workshop world than almost anyone. While leading the most prestigious workshops for Farafina and others, she has also been one of the most central event hosts and prize judges and inspiring examples for aspiring authors.

She takes on the workshop world in an interesting way in her own short story "Jumping Monkey Hill," first published in *Granta* magazine in 2008. It is instructive to interpret the story in relation to the conditions of the emergence of African literary culture that I have been charting here, to suggest that these conditions are not external to the text, but rather integral to what writers imagine and communicate as they position themselves within a given field.

As the story opens, creative writers arrive for their workshop retreat at a resort that has "the complacence of the well fed about it." Here they are quite lavishly wined and dined while receiving instruction from leader Edward Campbell – a white patron of the African literary arts with a lecherous eye and, despite boasting no evident credentials, strong ideas about what counts as representatively African. Edward founded the workshop, which is "funded graciously" by something called the Chamberlain Arts Foundation, funders also of a "Lipton African Writers' Prize." Participating writers hail from an array of African cities and they are expected to each produce one story "for possible publication in the *Oratory*," a journal Edward appears also to have control over. Adichie is clearly targeting, here, the close links between workshops, prizes, and publications – links that tend to empower particular key figures as gate-keepers and patrons within the African literary field.

This is observed through the point of view of Ujunwa, a young woman from Nigeria whose workshop story is an autobiographical account of taking a job at a bank and being forced to entertain wealthy men, even sexually, in order to secure their business. We gather that this story is, in an oblique way, also about the workshop itself. It features the effects of being in a position of having to do something you do not enjoy – the bank job, the sociality of the workshop scene – in order to get something that you do want, namely a livelihood. The parallels go even deeper. Edward is sexually interested in Ujunwa and does not work very hard to hide it, instead staring at her breasts constantly and making jokes about wanting her to "lie down" "for" him. She has to stomach his uncomfortable attention in order to survive the workshop; another writer opines sagely that "Edward was connected and could find them a London agent" and there is "no need to close the doors on opportunity."

At the end of Ujunwa's workshop story, which the participants read and comment upon as their time at the workshop is coming to a close, its protagonist achieves a complicated victory. She refuses to be sexual with a man in order to keep her rubbish job; so she is unemployed, but not compromised. Parallel again, Ujunwa too achieves a small victory as a workshop participant, as she gains the courage to say something about the limitations to Edward's conception of Africa. Standing up for a queer Zimbabwean writer when Edward wonders if "homosexual stories of this sort weren't reflective of Africa, really," she demands "Which Africa?" She also gets the pleasure of shocking Edward's wife Hillary, an animal rights activist who rails against poaching – indifferent to the poverty that moti-vates poachers but highly attentive to the plight of endangered apes and tuskless elephants, and hostile to whatever cultural practices might be involved ("They just used the private parts for charm," she laments). Ujunwa tells Hillary that her faux-ivory necklace, in fact purchased at the resort's giftshop, is perfectly real.

As it happens the workshop story that Edward likes best is the one that most conforms to the stereotype of African literary "poverty porn" fixated on war, violence, and suffering in "darkest Africa." Ujunwa observers that this particular story "was about the killings in Congo, from a militiaman's point of view, a man full of prurient violence." Edward is immediately sure that "it would be the lead story in the *Oratory*, that it was urgent and relevant" and "brought news." Ujunwa disagrees, describing it as "like a piece from *The Economist* with cartoon characters painted in." A further irony, then, that Edward finds Ujunwa's story unconvincing as a portrait of what real women experience in Nigeria. "It's never quite like that in real life, is it?" "Women are never victims in that sort of crude way," he says, "and certainly not in Nigeria. Nigeria has women in high positions. The most powerful cabinet minister is a woman." Another writer chimes in that he does not think a woman without other choices would really quit her job like she does in Ujunwa's story, and Edward adds that "The whole thing is implausible . . . This is agenda writing, it isn't a real story of real people." We know that the story is Ujunwa's true experience, though, and that she came to the workshop thinking she could pursue writing instead of banking, expecting something different, and instead finding . . . Edward Campbell. The story ends with her retreating from the sociality of the workshop to be alone in her cabin and perhaps call her mother – driving home the point that, in the form that she finds it, the writing workshop is intolerable, more a burden than a help. The point of the narration – both Adichie's and Ujunwa's – is to communicate the truth of her experience, no matter how little it accords with Edward's vision of African women – a vision that cannot even be reconciled with his own leering creepiness – no matter what her peers think most genuine to human behavior.

What does "Jumping Monkey Hill" do, then, with the power of the creative writing workshop as an institution mediating career success and networking opportunities? Certainly it does not make the hackneyed point that creative writing instruction channels or stifles creativity; and nor does it suggest that there is something basically wrong with all networks of prestige and esteem that give some writers access to the workshop circuit and thus to the connections that can ease one's path to success. The story's message rather is that the African literary workshop scene should not be run by white people who want to dictate what counts as authentic cultural experience. The leadership has to change, first, and the fact that there is a multiplicity of genuinely African stories should just be taken as a given. So the centrality of the workshop leader is not a problem, so long as the leader is the right person. Gatekeeping is not a problem if it is done in light of the correct perspectives. The paths to publication *will* be narrow; the only question is who will make them?

You might already be thinking from my description of the story that "Jumping Monkey Hill" repeats points Adichie makes in her popular TED Talk, also from 2009, on the danger of the single story, which has as of July 2020 been viewed more than 6.6 million times on YouTube. This talk has been widely embraced as a manifesto for contemporary African writers who seek to challenge limiting stereotypes about what is authentically African. In it, she remembers a professor she had as a student in the USA, who, quite like Edward Campbell, complained that Adichie's writing did not seem authentic to him. She talks about power – not the power of cultural elites, or the power of having been born into relative wealth, but the power that stories have to shape our perception of reality. She speaks of her own work of cofounding Farafina Trust as a response to this power: an effort to correct misperceptions about the realities of African life. She highlights that, against all the dreary stereotypes, people in Africa do continue to "nurse ambition" despite the odds stacked against them, and despite inept and indifferent governments – ambitions, in the examples she mentions, for excellence in filmmaking and in publishing, in education and writing. "Jumping Monkey Hill" reinforces this argument about nursing ambition by similarly imagining a young writer who aspires to something better – to literary writing – despite the odds, and whose experiences simply exceed what the white workshop leader is able to fathom, his "one story" being the tragic one of war-torn suffering Africa.

It is when we read the story in relation to the emergent networks of urban African literary control that we can see how it helps to explain and reinforce those networks, which powerfully concentrate acclaim and esteem, and are made up of writers such as Adichie who have achieved great success overseas, who have teaching posts in US university creative writing programs, who have agents and markets in New York and London, and who have won many prizes and accolades and become themselves the key prize adjudicators. The story is about this context. It works to ground Adichie's own status as one of the people with legitimate power to decide how workshops should be run and how good writing should be defined and evaluated. To use conventional Bourdieusian terminology, it helps to authorize those who authorize, in this instance reflecting and supporting a marked shift in the production of African literature toward local networks of African writers who are often working simultaneously as creative writing workshop teachers, readers of their peers' work, editors of journals, prize judges, event hosts, sought-after public speakers – scene makers, really, with significant power to influence new writing and promote the authors whose work they approve of.

Furthermore, and finally, the activity of scene-making and authority-granting is presented as nonproblematic because it is in the service of cultivation of something that is beyond reproach: literary culture. After all, as Adichie argues in "The Danger of a Single Story," reading makes you aware of others' experiences. The right stories "empower," "humanize," and "repair broken dignity" (2009). We are meant to accept that reading material pitched at an elevated level is both good as a sign of development, and good as a tool to use in furthering social and economic uplift toward a higher standard.

6 The Demotic Picaresque

The appearance of a new genre indicates that new social experiences were demanding expression. (Barber 2012, 12)

What, in turn, about that other cluster, a more demotic reading culture that is not much fixated on anything like the high literary? This entails many kinds of reading – reading for information and to navigate daily life, reading to practice for school, reading for transport, absorption and edification, and participation in reading events for the convivial occasion of a certain kind of sociality offered by being in common. There are generative connections and tensions between developmentalism and a more fitful, immediate, picaresque mode. We saw that the more developmentalist ideology equates reading, especially reading high literature, with progressive social development and the growth of human capital; in turn, I suggest, the picaresque is a more practical, functional, or survivalist style concerned with making do and finding what one needs to cope with the challenges of daily life. This is not a sophisticated schema, to be sure, and the categories are always overlapping and intersecting, as we shall see. Still, it is important to recognize their distinctness – because, in fact, the more elite sphere tends to be funded and developed as a way to attempt to manage the messy demotic sphere to which it is counterposed. Relative cultural elites are hailed and fostered as those who might help to channel – develop, again – illicit behaviors into productive activities in the more official, legal, book world.

English-language African writing in the more demotic and informal category is dynamic and lively. Its relative flourishing tells us something about the future of reading culture in general, even in the developed world, where cultivation of the high-literary sociolect was once more forceful than it is now, and where this cultivation has lost many of its dominant supports or seen serious decline – declines in funding for higher education, in anything like an affordable student loan, in funding for public library purchasing of new books, in disposable income, in the numbers of writers making their living as authors, and so much more.

There is now in this emergent position in the publishing world, perhaps even globally, a demotic reading culture fueled by smartphones, self-publishing, and social media. Here, for instance, very short micro-fiction or "flash fiction" is on the rise, alongside short digestible poems that have clear messages and are attached to vibrant social media celebrities like Rupi Kaur. There are books but not expensive paperbound objects, and phones being used for everything from downloads of digital text to arranging and archiving attendance at pop-up events. There are market stalls selling pirated and plagiarized books very cheaply. There are alternative types of payment for books via smartphone, like using mobile phone credits. And there is a remarkable expansion of the self-publishing niche, which intermingles with all of these other facets of the field, as people embrace platforms that allow them to simply upload their writing and hope for a readership.

This emergent scene has recently been studied in some detail by a project situated at Uppsala University in Sweden, led by Ashleigh Harris and Nicklas Hållén, called "African Street Literatures and the Future of Literary Form." Harris argues that "the published book is an unsustainable form for Africa's literary future" and states that there has already been "movement away from the book-commodity as the dominant form of literary production in Africa" (2019, 1). While African literary fiction is, as many have claimed, often "extroverted" and oriented towards a Western readership, there are demotic genres and forms that face inwards towards African social life. Harris and Hållén study what I want to describe as picaresque forms – forms of English reading that are not, in Annie McClanahan's terms (2019), "easily wrestled into more familiar narratives of development, education, and achievement." Writing about US-based TV shows focused on people working in the gig economy, McClanahan describes the picaresque as "the genre of unwaged work." She writes that "the picaresque's preference for the episodic over the continuous, parataxis over bildung, dispersal over development, and . . . fleeting spatial encounter over extended historical association makes it an apt form for describing the experiences of a population defined by exclusion, precarity, and superfluity rather than by any more stable, homogeneous, predictable coherence" (2019). What we see in the demotic reading sector in Africa are some of the formal consequences of this same precarity and superfluity: very short texts that are easy and cheap to acquire; and works produced, often informally, for small, unpredictable profit. A further point to emphasize here is how those in the more developmentalist camp, who as we have seen are interested in expanding readership and the book industries in Africa, are clearly threatened by some of what takes place in the informal sector and picaresque mode. They seem to want not just reading activity of whatever kind, but rather consumption of copyrighted products that have been sanctioned by the approved gatekeepers.

It is worth homing in on a few of the demotic genres and forms here, as the sites of a substantial dynamism in English reading culture. One of the most significant aspects of book culture right now, expanding in Africa and elsewhere, is self-publishing, which people with access to agents and official outlets are usually quick to dismiss and deride as unedited, messy, badly written, substandard and so on. Harris considers Nielsen BookScan data for sales of South African fiction between 2013 and 2017 in order to glimpse the extent of self-publishing's growing dominance. She points, first, to the low profits made by fiction publishers in South Africa during this period (2019, 9). Three of the biggest South African publishing houses, Jacana, Kwela Books, and Picador Africa, "sold on average across the three years between 2253 (Picador Africa), 10 226 (Jacana), and 11 386 (Kwela) fiction titles per year"; Harris notes in addition that Kwela's sales "dropped by more than half between 2015 (15 369 books sold) and 2017 (6948 books sold)." In 2016 Hlomu Publishing entered the market, selling 6556 copies in its first year, and going on to "take a profit of around 1,5 million ZAR in 2017," making it "the second largest seller of fiction in South Africa in 2017." Just a remarkable, aggressive new publishing house entering the field? Not quite. Because Hlomu Publishing is run by one author, Dudu Busani-Dube, "who started the company to self-publish her trilogy of romance novels" (2019, 9). Thus, sales of these three titles by this one author, which are mass market genre romance fiction, can best sales of fiction by nearly all other prominent South African publishers. Needless to say, this is a bit worrying to the traditional publishers, who are wondering how to stay standing in this new landscape.

Another of their notable worries is book pirates. Piracy poses a clear and often remarked-upon challenge to aspiring official publishers. Recent estimates in Nigeria for example suggest that illegal sales account for 75 percent of the book market. In Zimbabwe, an anti-piracy group, with stakeholders including publishers, booksellers, writers, and the police, received significant funding from UNESCO for a crackdown on piracy. Their position is that prospective writers simply will not bother trying to publish and copyright anything because they know that their work will be pirated. This anti-piracy group reported at the Zimbabwe International Book Fair in 2013 "on the growing problem of book piracy in the country, a problem that has only worsened" because of "access to mobile technologies and the ease with which texts can be digitally transferred" (Harris 2019, 7). The growing access to technology and the possibilities for wide distribution of texts are acknowledged here, but in a negative vein of complaint about illegal file sharing. Again, we see that it is not reading as such that is supported, but expansion of the industry's hold over reading materials.

Official bookstores have reported that they will refuse to reorder certain books because they could be so easily purchased in pirated copies just around the corner from the stores. To deter theft, publishers will provide the stores with doctored or ruined sample copies that are supposed to direct buyers to the bookstore counter to get the "real" book (Harris 2019, 6). Then even these ruined copies make their way into the illegal market, because in fact many readers do not care at all if the book which they are reading is not the perfect instance. And this is the rub for publishers. This split between the "real" book and the ruined fake can be mapped without much difficulty onto the other divisions I have been noting. There is a reader who can take pride in having purchased the official version approved by publisher and bookseller, perhaps at a nice bookstore in a new mall, and their pride depends on the entirety of the social fact of the extensiveness of available fakes. In turn, there is the reader who just wants something to read, perhaps picking up a pirated book at a bookstall because they recognize the author's name, and so enjoying that particular transactional utility of knowing they are reading a popular title but at a fraction of the price that others have paid.

And if one is looking for ease of access and low prices, again we see the relevance of self-publishing, and with the rising rates of adoption of mobile phones there has been a rise in what we might call smartphone literatures – meaning, simply, accessing reading material via smartphone, with the material itself designed to suit the reading situation. Harris and Hållén (forthcoming) point out that "At the end of 2015, almost half of the continent's population subscribed to mobile services, and approximately a quarter of all connections were mobile broadband connections." They write further that "migration to mobile broadband connections will likely continue in the coming years: it is estimated that the number of mobile broadband connections will triple in the period 2015–2020." There has been in this climate a remarkable growth in the area of flash fiction –which can be both read and written on smartphones and other handheld devices. There are many online literary forums now that feature short works, such as Flash Fiction Ghana, Words are Work, Brittle Paper, and Pulse. And there are competitions like the African Writing Prize for Flash Fiction and the 9Mobile Flash Fiction Competition.

OkadaBooks is a primary example of the emerging reading culture: a Nigerian website and mobile app that publishes works by unestablished writers, often self-published authors who simply upload their works and receive 70 percent of the profits from sales. The website states that the company is "named after the popular motorcycle taxis that are ubiquitous in Nigerian cities," and was conceived in response to the "traffic jam in the book distribution space in Nigeria" caused by "poor infrastructure of distribution and high printing costs" (Hållén 2018a, 37). In 2018 Hållén interviewed OkadaBooks' first employee, who explained founder Okechukwu Ofili's "frustrations trying to sell his books in Nigeria. He went from bookstore to bookstore, looking to get his books accepted. When these bookstores finally did [accept his books] and sold [them], it became difficult to get the money from the sale of his books; he spent months chasing the store owners around for his own money" (Hållén 2018b, 86). Ofili's experiences trying to make a living in the field "inspired his mission" to make it easier to publish and sell books in Nigeria and elsewhere (Hållén 2018b, 86). OkadaBooks started thus as a way to make the book-world hustle easier for authors. Not many users will make much money doing it, but the idea is that plenty will be able to find at least some readers with relative ease. Its website currently claims that it has serviced nearly 400,000 readers.

Users download books for free or at a modest price – roughly 50 cents to 2.50 CAD. These prices make texts accessible to readers who would not be able to afford officially printed copyright-protected books. The app allows readers to browse through categories such as Bestsellers, Business-minded, Girl Power, and Leadership. It also links to blog posts on topics such as how to pronounce challenging words, or "5 Benefits of Creative Writing to Help Your Children." I read a recent bestseller for early 2020, a self-published work, *Bizarre Entanglement* by Nky Omeka. Like many of the app's top sellers, it is a romance novel, in this case featuring a woman who, attempting to leave a bad home situation, is engaged to marry a wealthy abusive man. With the wedding date set, she meets someone who is kind and nurturing. Can he save her from her fate? It is 134 gripping pages; I will not spoil the ending. It sells for ₦350.00, or 1.35 CAD.

One final thing to mention in the picaresque network is street poetry, which takes place with little to no running costs and for little or no profit. It is not based around sales of discrete books, although as Harris and Hållén point out YouTube is making some of its usual predictable inroads there in commodifying videos of street poetry performances. In a forthcoming article, Harris and Hållén study Street Poetry Kenya, a small poetry collective that organizes events that are marketed by word-of-mouth and via social media. They do not have a formal event space or headquarters; the events are held in public space; they are held at a regular weekday and time, which can minimize promotion costs and makes the format of the event easily sustainable. There are no microphones, no amplifiers, and no seats for the audience – all keeping costs low, basically nil. They are free to attend. People capture videos with their phones and upload them to YouTube; this becomes an archive of performances, a way to be there without being there, and creates buzz for subsequent events. Like the other forms of emerging reading culture mentioned here, street poetry is affordable and accessible by design. It is available to people who may not have time, money, or training to sit and read a longer literary work. It is a post-print experience of reading that is also a site of enjoyable sociality.

7 Bildung *and* Picaresque

So far I have mapped quickly and schematically two fields here: on the one hand, the dominant matrix of the festival culture, development education, foundation-funded coteries, and the high-literary niche, all aligned roughly with cultivation and sale of paperbound books; and on the other hand the emergent niche of the entrepreneurial smartphone "flash" literature written for people on the move and looking for relatively short immersive experiences in reading. The relationship between these spaces is sometimes symbiotic and sometimes aversive, sometimes convivially overlapping and sometimes more clashing and colliding.

Esther de Bruijn has, for example, studied the way that Accra's quasi-legal "informal-sector print district of New Town" grew in response to a growing demand for inexpensive reading materials to supplement English-language training. She indicates that at its "nexus between 2005 and 2007, this locally produced and circulated informal-sector book industry saw sales in the range of 50,000 copies each week" (2018, 130). This surge was the product of market fiction producers cannily finding "gaps in the state provision of education" to "offer informal fixes to the contradictions at the core of national educational policy – the most pointed being the lack of adequate literature in schools" (2018, 133). There was official government messaging emphasizing the importance of education and of learning to read, but schools were underfunded, with cuts to education and prohibitive fees increasingly common from the early 1980s on.

Parents and children turned to market literature produced in the informal sector in response, where they found stories that had enough of what de Bruijn calls a didactic "architecture" (2018, 132) – stories of godliness and of commitment to professional success – that they were otherwise permitted to skirt the rules of formal business practice as well as of the official curriculum and the formal standards of "cultured" taste. In short, New Town's informal producers took advantage of the need for reading materials arising from public recognition of the importance of literacy – as those urged to "prioritize their children's education" were at the same time ill served by the formal industry and by the school system itself. Given the "youth bulge" has been identified as a demographic factor in many African cities, the pressures on the education system and the need for training in English are more acute now than ever. Though the concerted efforts of New Town's informal producers were dashed by the 2008 economic crisis, and have as far as I know not been matched since, readers by all means continue to find similarly "unruly" supplementary reading material at market stalls, or shared by friends, or in digital form.

An obvious example of the relationship between the official and the informal sectors being more aversive is what I have already mentioned – the effort of the official publishing world to control what is read, for example by cracking down on copyright infringement, and the way the development establishment that funds so many ventures will support this crackdown, to the detriment of the pirates, who it must be said perform a service vital to many readers. An example of the relationship being more symbiotic is, say, OkadaBooks making works by famous writers, such as Chimamanda Adichie, available for download very cheaply. They promote their company through this means. Such promotion is key because the success of the platform depends on how many users it can convince to sign on. The more users it has the more it will be able to help aspiring self-publishing authors find enough readers to make their writing pay at least a modest amount, and the more it will be able to facilitate sharing of texts in ways that make reading affordable for those otherwise restricted from it.

And an example of the relationship being more perhaps colliding and even appropriative is when the demotic picaresque vibe is used to market official print titles. Ephemeral market literature is a look, it turns out. Harris and Hållén give the cheeky example of the "hip urban-African aesthetic" of the New Generation African Poets series, published jointly by Slapering Hol Press in New York, the African Poetry Book Fund based in Lincoln, Nebraska, and the Poetry Foundation in Chicago. These are marketed to resemble chapbooks, with the look of a small press book, almost handmade. Chapbooks are popular for self-published titles and common in emergent African literary scenes. But these New Generation African Poets titles are produced by professional publishers, feature mainly well-positioned and prized writers, with backing from some of the biggest institutions in the field. Harris and Hållén (forthcoming) point out that "The texts are paginated, have ISBN numbers, are copyrighted, are professionally printed on high quality paper, with colour covers." They are also edited by Kwame Dawes and Chris Abani, well-established African writers who live in the USA and are based at US universities.

We can find a more substantial case of collision in what I turn to now – the accounts of Canadian volunteer writers and editors who traveled to Africa to help run workshops under the auspices of the CODE Burt Literary Awards. The Canadian Organization for Development through Education (CODE), started its programming in Africa with book donation schemes, before extending to library and literacy development and to a book prize for writers in the young adult category, and expanding also to work in the Caribbean and in Indigenous and Metis communities in Canada. The CODE Burt Award is designed to encourage local authors to write fiction for youth. It recognizes and celebrates worthy titles every year with generous monetary awards (up to 10,000 CAD). It also purchases significant quantities of the award-winning books – 2,000 to 2,500 copies are typical – and distributes them to schools and libraries, where teachers can then use them to help strengthen their students' literacy skills.[4] Until its funding was cut after the recent death of donor William Burt, it was offering an annual prize to authors of novels targeted at a young adult readership in four countries in African – Kenya, Tanzania, Ethiopia, and Ghana – with the addition in more recent years of a culminating prize for one top choice amongst all the respective national winners. The idea behind the prize was to cultivate the reading habit by making exciting fiction available to young readers who might otherwise find themselves confined to dry textbooks.

Retired commodities broker turned millionaire investor and philanthropist, William Burt had been involved with CODE as a donor and volunteer for some time. He founded the CODE Burt prize after traveling to Ethiopia in 2007 where, by his own account, he found one beat up copy of a book written for a younger audience at a library. One of the library's most popular titles, it

---

[4] Information about the CODE Burt Literary Awards is available on the CODE website, where readers can access annual reports and financial statements from 2008 to the present. I owe a great debt to CODE Burt program manager Lynn O'Rourke, who shared further materials with me, including the volunteer field reports that I quote from below. The volunteer reports are housed in the CODE offices in Ottawa, Canada.

was basically falling apart from over-appreciation and the absence of comparable titles. The CODE Burt Literary Awards would thus support the printing and distribution of books like it, with prizewinning titles transported to schools and other organizations. It would also serve to encourage local writers to try their hand at writing and specifically at writing fiction for young people – something that, without the lure of the prize money, they might otherwise never consider, even as a pastime. It must be noted that Burt made much of his money trading energy futures and petroleum stocks. Petroleum extraction and waste disposal have been hugely destructive in areas of Africa, most notoriously the Niger Delta, where the Nigerian government and multinational petroleum firms conspired to kill Ken Saro-Wiwa, himself a lauded writer who had led Ogoni resistance to the firms in the region. So, Burt's wealth was built upon the same dispossession and impoverishment to which CODE's literacy development work responds.

Burt's generous funding supported the appointment of Canadian writers to the judging panel; and, when they traveled to Africa, they ran several days of workshops for writers and editors. Their accounts of their trips offer telling details about the sort of literary economy that the CODE Burt Literary Award works within and fosters. The volunteer Canadian writers worry, for example, that the main motivation of those who come to participate in the workshop is not a passion for writing per se but instead simply an enterprising drive to win the prize. Often writers who have already won the prize are there again as participants, becoming familiar faces to the judges. Numerous authors have won the prize more than once, and when Canadian volunteers suggest restrictions on how many times one can win, the local representatives disagree on the grounds that one must not disincentivize submissions and punish success.

A volunteer working in Kenya in 2014 remarks that "it became clear to me that for many of the attendees the workshop was primarily a fact-finding mission, with the goal being: what is the formula for winning the Burt Award." Having led several days of workshops, he complains that participants would tend to ask frustratingly specific questions: "How long should sentences be? What do you consider the ideal entry point for a young adult story? What should be the best number of characters for a story for a 15-year-old? What should be the level and nature of tragedy in a children's story/novel?" They seem to fail to feel the spark of storytelling, viewing it instead as a technical exercise and focused on nitty-gritty details of what the prize judges will be looking for. Even worse, some volunteers worry: are the workshop participants mainly there for the food? They arrive late – the locals are notoriously indifferent to being punctual, reports laugh – but seem in no hurry to leave after 4:30 p.m. when "new plate loads of sandwiches and sweets and coffee and tea would be brought it." "As dilatory as they'd been in coming," one observer quips, "no one seemed in any hurry to leave."

The same charges extend to local publishers: volunteer reports wonder if publishers are annoyed at having to spend time with titles that have not won yet; they do not want to waste their time editing books that will not win the prize, and in some cases they have failed to honor contracts to publish books that were nominated but didn't win, or that ended up runners-up at second or third. Nor, some complain, do these publishers share the production values of the Canadian judges and workshop leaders. Where is their passion for the craft? In the early days of the prize, writers submitted their manuscripts directly, without the intervention of publishers. The idea was – and this usually played out – that winning manuscripts could then be placed with publishers with relative ease, on the strength of their winning status and funding from CODE. This was later changed, however, and manuscripts submitted to the prize arrived from publishers, who were meant to have done some work to improve the quality of the manuscripts, but often had at not – or at least not to the standards of the writers serving on the judging panel and running the workshops. One report recounts: "The hope was that publishers would have done some editing of the works before submitting, but this doesn't appear to have been done. (At the publishers' meeting later in the week, one publisher remarked that publishers were reluctant to spend a lot of editorial energy on a manuscript that might not win.)"

As a result, due to the structure of the prize and its place within the surrounding field, the judges end up working as the winning manuscripts' editors. They offer feedback on the manuscripts and emphasize that they will be worthy of a prize only after the changes that they recommend have been made. Sometimes edits are made and sometimes they are not; on at least one occasion a volunteer report states a prize would be withheld if there was a failure to edit to the judges' standard: "in our comments to the publisher we directed that the author himself must supply the missing chapter – in other words, complete his story – as a condition of its achieving a place in the award list."

Certain refrains are evident across the volunteers' reports: they lament an apparent lack of concern for quality; note little evidence even that the works have been copyedited; object to annoyingly overt moral lessons ("Didacticism – sometimes in the form of barely concealed lectures – was, to my mind, one of the biggest problems with most of the pieces"); find basic grammatical errors throughout and frequent typos; and see little evidence especially of substantive structural editing, the kind that might result for instance from an editor making a critical intervention suggesting that an author remove or add an element of the work or reconsider sequencing, character development, the presence and nature of the moral lessons, and so on.

In fact it could be said that for the volunteer workshop leaders, absence of commitment to substantive editing and to a real symbiotic working relationship between editor and author becomes one of the key signs of the local industry's impoverishment: the lodestar for a soundly developed literary publishing industry, it seems to be utterly missing in most of the cases on hand as the judges make their decision. The persistent didacticism of the submissions is relevant here also: local judges seem to basically require heavily moral storytelling, while reports from Canadian volunteers almost always complain about it. One volunteer registers his hatred of the idea that the work of the judges and workshop leaders might be that of "Tailoring the story to our needs" – "a phrase that sends authorial shivers down my spine." The same judge suggests that his favorite title was not selected to win because it was too morally ambiguous, while the winning title was the "safest" and the "gatekeeper's choice." For these commentators, at least, a more respectable literary field would thus feature not these sanctimonious judges telling mendicant writers how to win, but rather symbiosis between trained creative talent and dedicated, perspicacious editors, with all players embracing a healthy ambivalence about using literature as a tool for moral instruction.

This is not what the CODE Burt Literary Awards foster at all, of course – and nor could they be expected to. Despite the narrative that they sell to donors, given all the other constraints detailed elsewhere in these pages, CODE cannot actually sponsor the gradual expansion of a dedicated leisure readership and the emergence of a more fully fledged literary culture serving young fiction readers. Instead the award is conducive to the fitful survival of a niche culture of reading and writing entirely structured by the prize itself: a small field of entrepreneurial applicants vying for this particular prize, writing the sorts of books that can win, and a small niche of publishers willing to put the work out because it has the backing of a Canadian development organization. One volunteer goes so far as to call the whole operation "a cash pursuit for a favoured few" – and this seems not an unfair assessment. Because while the larger developmentalist aims are not in any clear way being met, a small network of interested writers and publishers with close ties to the prize – to each other, to judges, to workshop leaders and so on – are managing to get something out of the endeavor, some "side hustle," as a recent prize recipient jokingly described it.

What does a prizewinning book look like? *Finding Colombia* by Kinyanjui Kombani (2018) makes a nice example. Kombani has been nominated for the CODE Burt Award several times and has won more than once. He is a professional banker and entrepreneur who writes as a hobby, though backed by the distinction of degrees from Kenyatta University in theater and creative writing. When asked in a recent interview what the prize means to him, he starts by mentioning the generous prize-money, and then remarks that having to travel because of his writing makes him feel like a real author rather than an amateur.

Tellingly, though, he would not consider leaving his stable job to make a living as a professional author – because despite all the efforts being made to develop the field, including by CODE itself, that is still not a feasible option. He is instead committed to his personal brand: "the banker who writes" (Oxford University Press EA 2018). This makes perfect sense. The money is an unpredictable prize, not remuneration from book sales; and indeed, as we have seen, few publishers are interested in fiction and even fewer want to take risks on untried talent. Even Kombani's publisher, Oxford University Press East Africa, only has literature as a small concern; its focus is school textbooks and other educational nonfiction titles. He is one of the fortunate few fiction writers to find a path into the industry – fortunate, too, in that Oxford University Press East Africa is one of the most established and successful presses in Africa. As we have seen OUP has operated in Africa since the colonial period, and though its management is now local it still has the foundation of the wealth of the parent company to fall back on. It is also heavily tied into state educational planning and curricula design and its main publishing offering is textbooks to students at all stages of learning. *Finding Colombia* is a "Starlit reader" – so one of a series of fictional titles aimed at learning readers, intended as lively prompts to their reading practice that feature both appealing age-appropriate stories and examples of sound grammatical prose. A perfect choice for a CODE Burt Literary Award then, firmly in line with the ethos of the prize. It is not the only Oxford University Press Starlit reader to have won.

The story itself also offers compatible messaging on sound development. Protagonist Lex is living on the streets as a drug addict, until officers from the Anti-Drugs Agency pick him up and force him to work as an under-cover agent tracking down a notorious drug dealer called Colombia. These police basically blackmail and entrap him; they are not appealing figures by any measure. However, because Colombia is thought to be hiding in a rehabilitation center, that is where they send Lex, and it is there that Lex is able to access what he really needs: help to overcome his addiction and set out on the path toward a productive life. At the story's close he decides to stay on in the rehabilitation center, even after the Anti-Drugs Agency has taken Colombia away, hoping to recover and then to help others like him overcome addiction.

This is the end of his story, but not the book: turning to the final page, one finds an Oxford University Press caution against pirated and plagiar-ized books. As you would help the police catch a drug lord, help the publishing industry police menacing book pirates. Crime is crime is crime. It is good for business for Oxford University Press and other official presses, of course, if people buy their books, which are substantially pricier than pirated copies; but it is good also for everyone to obey the law, as we have learned from Lex's story. (See Figure 3.)

"Book Piracy and Plagiarism are Crimes. Beware of both!" In case you did not realize that you too might be engaged in the sort of criminal activity

Figure 3 A warning against piracy and plagiarism. From *Finding Colombia* by Kinyanjui Kombani ©Oxford University Press East Africa. Reproduced by permission of Oxford University Press East Africa (Pty) Ltd.

cautioned against in the novel. You might be reading a pirated book, or a plagiarized one, in either case betraying the legal ownership that an author has over their copyright. The list of characteristics to look for turns the reader into an officer of the law, attuned to the risks posed by "inferior production quality" and "substandard appearance." Working with Oxford University Press, they can root out and turn in suspect books, and help to maintain copyright security. I cannot help but add here that in 2012 the World Bank fined Oxford University Press and debarred two of its subsidiaries from operating in Africa for a period of three years, after finding that the companies bribed government officials to secure textbook contracts linked to educational projects that had World Bank financing (see Vasagar 2012). In this light, their activities are more about monopoly than legality. Using bribes to secure contracts, and cracking down on piracy, are equally efforts to secure Oxford University Press's market dominance.

In *Finding Colombia*'s anti-piracy notice, the list of "substandard" things to watch for neatly complements the complaints of CODE volunteers about the sorts of texts they are sometimes presented with – texts to which publishers less responsible than Oxford University Press have failed to add any value, which as a result do not meet the standards of a developed, legally regulated publishing industry committed to fine, sturdy, error-free objects. In this way Oxford University Press East Africa, along with *Finding Colombia*, "the banker who writes," and the CODE Burt Literary Awards form a matrix connecting copyrighted official press books to sound moral law-abiding activities and personal and social development. Well-designed books produced relatively expensively are not only nice to have; they are moral objects bespeaking a proper regard for good behavior and productive citizenship. In their commitment to production quality and laments about the absence of substantive editing, the Canadian CODE Burt Award volunteers write against the more desultory commitments apparently reflected in the "substandard" submissions they receive and in the dilatory or mercenary attitudes of some of the workshop participants and partnered publishers.

We see then the tension between developmentalist goals and a more fitful enterprising ethos play out within the African literary field. We see once more how the customary analytical habit of pitting mainstream versus independent, big versus small, and economically motivated versus authentic culture, makes little sense here. Unlike in the literary industries in the wealthier economies, here much of the funding is from private foundations and foreign charities, where readers are finding materials at school, rarely paying for books, and even more rarely paying full price for "legit" press books, and writers are doing other jobs besides – whether they are making ends meet however they can, or enjoying the fruits of the relative wealth and high cultural status that one would already need to possess in order for them to access the skills required to write in the prizewinning style.

It is interesting in this respect to compare *Finding Colombia* to a title Esther de Bruijn studies in her work on the Ghanaian informal-sector market literature that arose in the mid-2000s to serve notice-readers who could not pursue regular instruction or school or whose schools had too few books. (See Figures 4 and 5)

The Wicked Mother, published by a firm called Knowledge Source Publishing, "promises with its 'For Schools' marketing splash that it is appropriate for adoption into the reading periods of educational institutions" (de Bruijn 2018, 131). Yet the cover's sensational horror of a mother attacking her child, rendered in a hand-drawn style, sets it apart quite clearly from an officially sanctioned prizewinning work like *Finding Colombia*. The publisher was part of Accra's informal economy; its books were not sold in stores where sales would be tracked by barcodes and ISBN numbers. Sales occurred near schools, and *The Wicked Mother* does what it needs to do to count as pedagogically appropriate: its "overt lesson is that keeping a focus on moral uprightness pays off even for the victim of extreme parental abuse" (de Bruijn 2018, 132). Yet its aesthetic is ultimately one of what de Bruijn calls "didactic sensationalism" (2018, 133); in arriving at its message, it incorporates many references to popular cultural practices, and a sensational plot line in which the mother's racism against her darker-skinned son – the story's protagonist – comes to a sinister end. Though she has arranged to deliver him to men who plan to use his head in a ritual, he has been delayed while listening to a preacher in the market square, who is intoning, "*All things go well for those who trust in the LORD, for the LORD knows his children*"; when he eventually arrives on the scene he finds instead his own twin brother, who is lighter skinned, murdered and headless; and the mother dies of grief upon hearing the news. All is not lost for the protagonist though – the preacher's words are a portent, and he goes forth as a motherless child of God instead, eventually becoming a medical doctor with a middle-class family and home.

Figure 4 Cover image from *The Wicked Mother*. Reproduced from Esther de Bruijn, 2018, "A Permissive Frame for Unrulyness," 131

The Wicked Mother takes advantage of the need for reading materials to supplement literacy instruction, as *Finding Colombia* does. It fills a gap that exists because of schools having inadequate textbook resources. But *The Wicked Mother* is more cheaply made and sold, and circulates in the informal sector as a quasi-legal object that traffics in sensation even while maintaining its pedagogical moralism; *Finding Colombia* is a deliberate counter to

Figure 5 Cover image from *Finding Colombia* by Kinyanjui Kombani ©Oxford University Press East Africa. Reproduced by permission of Oxford University Press East Africa (Pty) Ltd.

work like it. It is a legally sanctioned, copyright protected, sturdily made object whose success is not dependent on market sales because it is backed by charitable donations, printed and published by one of the most established brands in African publishing – a brand whose identity is thoroughly linked to children's education and literacy.

Though well beyond the scope of the present inquiry, one notes how fruitful it could be to think in a more sustained historical way about the tensions and overlaps between developmentalist and picaresque print modes. For example, we could compare salacious market literatures to something like

Itan Igbesi Aiye Emi Ṣẹgilọla (*The Life Story of Me, Ṣẹgilọla*) – a work that was first serialized in a newspaper in the 1920s, and that has been described by Karin Barber (2012) as the first Yoruba novel. The African newspaper press had its origins in the nineteenth century in Christian missionary work, was taken up by colonial governments, and was also expanded and deployed by an anglicized elite who saw themselves as propagators of moral reform (see also Peterson & Hunter 2016). Indeed, the newspaper can be said to be one of the forms that, in its era of expansion, solidified the link between print culture and moral reform. Yet newspapers were also often unruly and cacophonous. Many operated in the informal sector, assembled by scrappy editors living hand to mouth, with little respect for copyright and liberal borrowings from other newspapers. Barber writes that most of the English and Yoruba newspapers that flourished in the early twentieth century:

> were one-man bands or very small businesses, and even the most successful had meagre resources; they could not afford to run a staff of investigative reporters or fact-gatherers. Much of the content of all the papers was opinion and editorializing; there was much reprinting and culling from other papers; much space was given to gossip and social news about the comings and goings of the tiny and highly visible elite. Entire sermons and political speeches could be reproduced in all of them, as well as official notices and government communications. (2016, 155)

Barber describes *The Life Story of Me, Ṣẹgilọla* as a work that carefully mediated these competing desires. It was, as in the case of *The Wicked Mother*, that same kind of "permissive frame for unruliness," to use de Bruijn's words, balancing sensationalist details against moral guidance, at once hailing and managing new readers. Here again, then, we see that the terminology pitting autonomous versus heteronomous print cultures, or restricted versus mass production, would not quite suffice. It fails to train our vision on the seeking of power and control – on fears of immorality and illegality driving the cultivation of emerging readers as responsible, moral citizens participating in an expanding legal marketplace.

8 Conclusion

This Element has emphasized the dependence of African literary development on contemporary social and economic realities. I suggested that it is useful to think a bit schematically at first, positing two fields that are separable though nevertheless thoroughly enmeshed with each other in important ways. One field is developmentalist, often funded by international agencies and private foundations, and invested in a bildung in which an encounter with reading – especially reading of more elevated materials – is a stepping-stone on a path toward improved personhood, improved life chances, general betterment of oneself and one's situation. In this field officials and practitioners make efforts to grow the official industry in the form of opening new legal businesses, printing more copyrighted works in greater numbers, getting more people to read official press books. The other field is more precarious. It features not a bildung but a survivalist picaresque, built upon episodic transfer of goods for money – it is more about getting by in "the hustle." It is less oriented toward development of the formal book industries, less worried about supporting legal businesses and organizations. It is more unsure about the legitimacy of the legitimate, and less attached, perhaps, to the "perfect" forms of well-made objects free of errors. Not because readers in the informal sector are not familiar with the standards of sound material appearance and grammatical writing – of course many very much are, and will gladly buy better books if they can. But many readers by necessity make do with what is available and will choose a cheaper book over a more perfect specimen.

To return to a mantra from cultural materialism: literature's forms change as social conditions of production change. Literature is a manifestation of social relationships, needs, capacities and constraints. New modes of reading culture have been emerging in relation to immiserating contemporary conditions. In the developmentalist milieu, the basic fact of limited local production of books is key, and there is foundation funding for development of niche cultural producers whose works sell far more abroad than at home. This funding comes to them in part because they are meant to be cultivated as a learned class that can shape what is acceptable – "civil" and "democratic" – in discussion of Africa's cultural and political futures. There is funding also for organizations that engage in efforts to train young writers in modes of expression that might help them channel unease, release tensions, and find work. In turn in the more informal milieu, there is the emergence of forms of writing that respond to the conditions of harried life, that take advantage of mobile phone adoption, that share and pirate and plagiarize to maximize access and minimize price.

I have highlighted how these fields intersect and interrelate, both in conflictual and in dependent ways. It may strike you that perhaps the most important area of overlap between these fields is of a significantly higher order than any effort to cultivate the reading habit: the former is meant to help manage the alarming social worlds and horizons of the latter, to for instance push radical literatures to the edge of acceptability, to maintain faith in the effort to aspire to success ("to nurse ambition") in market terms, to maintain faith in liberal capitalist development as a possibility for Africa and a way of solving the world's social problems. As Annie McClanahan writes, the figure of the picaro represents a threat to the social order precisely insofar as she is "protean, canny, and increasingly typical" (2019). Those working in a developmentalist vein work not just to foster literacy but to control what and how the newly literate, who are emerging in the growing megacities, go about reading. Perhaps it was ever thus in cultivation of reading – that there is always another goal, enmeshed within a broader history of class struggle, that is also being pursued where reading in English is being promoted, shaped, and aspired to.

The facts of urban life, which find people marshaling and managing their resources and searching for work, whether formal or informal, have been more effective instigations to English reading than the work of development agencies. Official culture hardly captures the whole of expressive life, though it does have the power of command over media as well as institutions of higher education and the interpretive apparatuses on offer there. The conditions for readers in Africa today are the conditions that many elsewhere also inhabit, and they are also a bellwether, as others will be finding themselves there before too long. On the high-literary end, we see diminishing state-based supports for reading, little free uninterrupted time, work blending into and consuming leisure time, and less and less money for books; and on the demotic end, we find harried life in un- and underemployment, shift and gig work, the scramble for competencies like English literacy in the search for work in cities, and the need for short bits of entertaining relief that promise uplift and amusement.

Given growing wealth disparities and spreading un- and underemployment, and attacks on the cultivation of leisured cultural consumption, the characteristic schema pitting autonomous versus heteronomous fields or restricted versus mass cultures, is losing its force. Replace it, then, with attention to small dominant sphere propped up by private monied interests struggling to maintain some composure and control in light of the emerging dynamism of more popular forces and forms. This is a relevant framework for study of reading cultures in general, perhaps, including in the "advanced" (de-developing) economies. There too we can expect to see decreasing private-sector activity coupled with increasing small press localist literary niches that see themselves as threatened and beleaguered. These will argue for and receive philanthropic donor funding on the grounds that they support threatened ideals of civic personhood and "literary activism" against state and market indifference. In turn, at the same time, we will see more and more of that picaresque reading activity that is hurried and practical – reading and writing where and how you can, often outside of formal economies or facilitated by platforms that allow for minimal price and minimal risk.

References

Abdulaziz, M. H. & Osinde, K. (1997). Sheng and Engsh: Development of Mixed Codes among the Urban Youth in Kenya. *International Journal of the Sociology of Language*, 125, 43–63. DOI: https://doi.org/10.1515/ijsl.1997.125.43.

Adichie, C. (2006). Jumping Monkey Hill. *Granta* (2 October). https://granta.com/jumping-monkey-hill.

Adichie, C. (2009). The Danger of a Single Story. www.ted.com/talks/chimamanda_ngozi_adichie_the_danger_of_a_single_story.

Altick, R. (1957). *The English Common Reader: A Social History of the Mass Reading Public 1800–1900*. Chicago: University of Chicago Press.

Barber, K. (2012). *Print Culture and the First Yoruba Novel: I. B. Thomas's "Life Story of Me, Segilola" and Other Texts*. Leiden and Boston: Brill.

Barber, K. (2016). Experiments with Genre in Yoruba Newspapers of the 1920s. In D. R. Peterson, E. Hunter, and S. Newell, eds., *African Print Cultures: Newspapers and their Publics in the Twentieth Century*. Ann Arbor: University of Michigan Press, pp. 151–178.

Behrstock, J. (1975). National Book Development Councils in Africa: A Report by Unesco Secretariat. In E. Oluwasanmi et al., eds., *Publishing in Africa in the Seventies*. Ile-Ife: University of Ife Press, pp. 78–88.

Benanav, A. (2019). Automation and the Future of Work – 1. *New Left Review*, 119, 5–38.

Bourdieu, P. (1983). The Field of Cultural Production, or: The Economic World Reversed. *Poetics*, 12, 311–356.

Carmody, P. (2012). The Informationalization of Poverty in Africa? Mobile Phones and Economic Structure. *Information Technologies and International Development*, 8(3), 1–17.

Chakava, H. (2008). African Publishing: From Ile-Ife, Nigeria, to the Present. In H. Zell, ed., *Publishing, Books & Reading in Sub-Saharan Africa: A Critical Bibliography*. Lochcarron: Hans Zell Publishing, pp. xxxvii-xlx.

Chakava, H. [1992] (2019). Kenyan Publishing: Independence and Dependence. In C. Davis, ed., *Print Cultures: A Reader in Theory and Practice*. London: Red Globe Press, pp. 203–209.

Davis, C. (2013). *Creating Postcolonial Literature: African Writers and British Publishers*. London: Palgrave.

de Bruijn, E. (2018). A Permissive Frame for Unruliness: The Educational Structures of Ghanaian Market Fiction. *Journal of the African Literature Association*, 12(2), 129–152. DOI: https://doi.org/10.1080/21674736.2018.1507407.

Durkheim, E. (1893). *De la division du travail social*. Paris: Félix Alcan.

Dyer-Witheford, N. (2015). *Cyber-Proletariat: Global Labour in the Digital Vortex*. London: Pluto Press.

Dyssou, N. (2017). An Interview with Ngũgĩ wa Thiong'o. *Los Angeles Review of Books* (23 April): https://lareviewofbooks.org/article/an-interview-with-ngugi-wa-thiongo.

Eatough, M. (2019). The Critic as Modernist: Es'kia Mphahlele's Cold War Literary Criticism. *Research in African Literatures*, 50(3), 136–156. DOI: https://doi.org/10.2979/reseafrilite.50.3.10.

Ede, A. (2015). Narrative Moment and Self-Anthropologizing Discourse. *Research in African Literatures*, 46(3), 112–129. DOI: https://doi.org/10.2979/reseafrilite.46.3.112.

EF. (2020a). English Proficiency Index: Africa: www.ef.com/ca/epi/regions/africa.

EF. (2020b). English Proficiency Index: Nigeria: www.ef.com/ca/epi/regions/africa/nigeria.

Ferguson, K. (2013). *Top Down: The Ford Foundation, Black Power, and the Reinvention of Racial Liberalism*. Philadelphia: University of Pennsylvania Press.

Ford Foundation. (2007). Ford Foundation's Longstanding Commitment Improves Lives in Eastern Africa. *Philanthropy News Digest* (31 July): https://philanthropynewsdigest.org/news/ford-foundation-s-long standing-commitment-improves-lives-in-eastern-africa.

Ford Foundation. (2020). Our Work Around the World: www.fordfounda tion.org/our-work-around-the-world/eastern-africa/history.

Goke-Pariola, A. (1993). *The Role of Language in the Struggle for Power and Legitimacy in Africa*. New York: The Edwin Mellen Press.

Griswold, W. (2000). *Bearing Witness: Readers, Writers, and the Novel in Nigeria*. Princeton: Princeton University Press.

Hållén, N. (2018a). OkadaBooks and the Poetics of Uplift. *English Studies in Africa*, 61(2), 36–48. DOI: https://doi.org/10.1080/00138398.2018.1540152.

Hållén, N. (2018b). Manoeuvring Through the Traffic Jam: A Conversation with Magnus Okeke About OkadaBooks and Digital Publishing in Nigeria. *English Studies in Africa*, 61(2), 86–90. DOI: https://doi.org/10.1080/00138398.2018.1540158.

Harris, A. (2018). Introduction: African Street Literatures and the Global Publishing Go-Slow. *English Studies in Africa*, 61(2), 1–8. DOI: https://doi.org/10.1080/00138398.2018.1540173.

Harris, A. (2019). Hot Reads, Pirate Copies, and the Unsustainability of the Book in Africa's Literary Future. *Postcolonial Text*, 14(2), 1–15.

Harris, A, & N. Hållén. African Street Literature: A Method for Emergent Form beyond World Literature. Forthcoming in *Research in African Literatures*. In Press.

Huggan, G. [2001]. (2019). African Literature/Anthropological Exotic. In C. Davis, ed., *Print Cultures: A Reader in Theory and Practice*. London: Red Globe Press, pp. 210–216.

Julien, E. (2006). The Extroverted African Novel. In F. Moretti, ed., *The Novel: History, Geography and Culture*, Vol. I. Princeton: Princeton University Press, pp. 667–700.

Kiguru, D. (2016). Literary Prizes, Writers' Organisations and Canon Formation in Africa. *African Studies*, 75(2), 202–214. DOI: https://doi.org/10.1080/00020184.2016.1182317.

Kombani, K. (2018). *Finding Colombia*. Nairobi: Oxford University Press East Africa.

Kotei, S. I. A. (1981). *The Book Today in Africa*. Paris: UNESCO.

Krishnan, M. & K. Wallis. Podcasting as Activism and/or Entrepreneurship: Cooperative Networks, Publics and African Literary Production. Forthcoming in *Postcolonial Text*. In Press.

Lizzaríbar Buxó, C. (1998). Something Else Will Stand Beside It: The African Writers Series and the Development of African Literature. PhD Thesis, Harvard University.

McClanahan, A. (2019). TV and Tipworkification. *post45* (10 January): http://post45.research.yale.edu/2019/01/tv-and-tipworkification.

Möller, J. & B. le Roux. (2017). Implementing Constitutional Language Provisions through the Indigenous Language Publishing Programme. *South African Journal of African Languages*, 37(2), 203–209. DOI: https://doi.org/10.1080/02572117.2017.1378274.

Mpofu, P. & A. Salawu. (2018). Re-examining the Indigenous Language Press in Zimbabwe: Towards Developmental Communication and Language Empowerment. *South African Journal of African Languages*, 38(3), 293–302. DOI: https://doi.org/10.1080/02572117.2018.1518036.

Newell, S. (2002). Introduction. In S. Newell, ed. *Readings in African Popular Fiction*. Bloomington. Indiana University Press, pp. 1–10.

Newell, S. (2006). *West African Literatures: Ways of Reading*. Oxford: Oxford University Press.

Ngũgĩ wa Thiong'o. (1986). *Decolonising the Mind: The Politics of Language in African Literature*. London: Heinemann.

Obiechina, E. (1973). *An African Popular Literature: A Study of Onitsha Market Pamphlets*. Cambridge: Cambridge University Press.

Ochiagha, T. (2015). *Achebe and Friends at Umuahia: The Making of a Literary Elite*. Suffolk: Boydell & Brewer Ltd.

Owoeye, O.K. & S.A. Dada. (2015). Creativity and Translation in Nigerian Literature: Yoruba Authors in Focus. *Journal of West African Languages*, 42(1), 107–123.

Oxford University Press EA. (2018). #FindingColombia live stream with the award winning author Kinyanjui Kombani and Oxford University Press East Africa, General Manager, John Mwazemba, 28 September: www.facebook.com/OxfordUniversityPressEA/videos/1139857622845714.

Peterson, D. R. & E. Hunter. (2016). Print Culture in Colonial Africa. In D. R. Peterson, E. Hunter & S. Newell, eds., *African Print Cultures: Newspapers and their Publics in the Twentieth Century*. Ann Arbor: University of Michigan Press, pp. 1–48.

Rathgeber, E-M. (1985). The Book Industry in Africa, 1973–1983: A Decade of Development? In P. Altbach et al., eds., *Publishing in the Third World: Knowledge and Development*. Portsmouth: Heinemann, pp. 55–75.

Rodney, W. (1972). *How Europe Underdeveloped Africa*. Dakar: Pambazuka Press.

Rodríguez, D. (2019). "Nuance" as Carceral Worldmaking: A Response to Darren Walker. *Abolition* (28 September): https://abolitionjournal.org/nuance-as-carceral-worldmaking-a-response-to-darren-walker/

Simmel, G. [1903] (1971). The Metropolis and Mental Life. In D. N. Levine, ed., *Georg Simmel on Individuality and Social Forms*. Chicago: University of Chicago Press, pp. 324–339.

Smith, K. (1977). *The Impact of Transnational Book Publishing on Intellectual Knowledge in Less Developed Countries*. Paris: UNESCO.

Strauhs, D. (2013). *African Literary NGOs: Power, Politics, and Participation*. London: Palgrave.

UNESCO. (2020). UNESCO eAltas of Literacy. https://tellmaps.com/uis/literacy/#!/tellmap/-601865091.

Vasagar, J. (2012). Oxford University Press fined £1.9m over bribery by African subsidiary firms. *Guardian* (3 July): www.theguardian.com/law/2012/jul/03/oxford-university-press-fined-bribery.

Wallis, K. (2018). Exchanges in Nairobi and Lagos: Mapping Literary Networks and World Literary Space. *Research in African Literatures*, 49(1), 163–186. DOI: 10.2979/reseafrilite.49.1.10.

Walker, D. (2019). In Defense of Nuance. Equals Change Blog, Ford Foundation (19 September): www.fordfoundation.org/ideas/equals-change-blog/posts/in-defense-of-nuance.

Zell, H. (2018). Publishing in African Languages: A Review of the Literature. Pre-print version. www.academia.edu/36334936/Publishing_in_African_Languages_A_Review_of_the_Literature.

Cambridge Elements $^{\equiv}$

Publishing and Book Culture

SERIES EDITOR
Samantha Rayner
University College London

Samantha Rayner is a Reader in UCL's Department of Information Studies. She is also Director of UCL's Centre for Publishing, co-Director of the Bloomsbury CHAPTER (Communication History, Authorship, Publishing, Textual Editing and Reading) and co-editor of the Academic Book of the Future BOOC (Book as Open Online Content) with UCL Press.

ASSOCIATE EDITOR
Leah Tether
University of Bristol

Leah Tether is Professor of Medieval Literature and Publishing at the University of Bristol. With an academic background in medieval French and English literature and a professional background in trade publishing, Leah has combined her expertise and developed an international research profile in book and publishing history from manuscript to digital.

ABOUT THE SERIES

This series aims to fill the demand for easily accessible, quality texts available for teaching and research in the diverse and dynamic fields of Publishing and Book Culture. Rigorously researched and peer-reviewed Elements will be published under themes, or 'Gatherings'. These Elements should be the first check point for researchers or students working on that area of publishing and book trade history and practice: we hope that, situated so logically at Cambridge University Press, where academic publishing in the UK began, it will develop to create an unrivalled space where these histories and practices can be investigated and preserved.

Cambridge Elements ≡

Publishing and Book Culture
Colonial and Post-Colonial Publishing

Gathering Editor: Caroline Davis

Caroline Davis is Senior Lecturer in the Oxford International Centre for Publishing at Oxford Brookes University. She is the author of *Creating Postcolonial Literature: African Writers and British Publishers* (Palgrave, 2013), the editor of *Print Cultures: A Reader in Theory and Practice* (Macmillan, 2019) and co-editor of *The Book in Africa: Critical Debates* (Palgrave, 2015).

ELEMENTS IN THE GATHERING

A full series listing is available at: www.cambridge.org/EPBC

Printed in the United States
By Bookmasters